CHARLES SIMEON

CHARLES SIMEON
(From the painting by Sir William Beechey)

GREAT ANGLICANS

CHARLES SIMEON
(1759–1836)

Essays Written in Commemoration of his Bi-Centenary
by Members of the Evangelical Fellowship
for Theological Literature

EDITED BY

ARTHUR POLLARD

AND

MICHAEL HENNELL

LONDON
S · P · C · K
1964

First published in 1959
Re-issued in this series 1964
S.P.C.K.

Holy Trinity Church
Marylebone Road
London N.W.1
Made and printed in Great Britain by
William Clowes and Sons, Limited, London and Beccle.

Contents

ACKNOWLEDGEMENTS

Thanks are due to the following for permission to include copyright material:

the Cambridge University Press (Charles Smyth: *Simeon and Church Order*).
William Collins, Sons and Co. (R. Coupland: *Wilberforce*).
Longmans, Green and Co. (A. M. Ramsey: *The Gospel and the Catholic Church*).

REFERENCES

W. Carus, *Memoirs of the Life of the Rev. Charles Simeon*, 1847, is referred to throughout as "Carus".
A. W. Brown, *Recollections of the Conversation Parties of the Rev. Charles Simeon*, 1863, is referred to as "Brown".
Simeon's sermons and sermon-outlines in *Horae Homileticae* are referred to by number and title.

Foreword

CHARLES SIMEON was born at Reading on 24 September 1759. He died in Cambridge on 13 November 1836. In the Cambridge to which he went as an undergraduate in 1779 he spent his whole life, for fifty-four years of it being the Vicar of Holy Trinity Church. In 1936 the centenary of his death was commemorated, not without some public notice. This volume of essays is part of the tribute that will be presented during the year which sees the bicentenary of his birth.

There is, of course, always a danger that such a tribute may become little else than an artificial attempt to resurrect some unfamiliar history with a view to extracting from it some edifying moral. And it is at least possible that suspicious minds will view this tribute as one more attempt to exploit history in the interests of ecclesiastical partisanship. The contributors to this volume hope that the reader will discover that the danger has been avoided and that the suspicion, if entertained, will prove to be without foundation.

The question may, however, be asked and not without reason—"Has Charles Simeon, his life and his work, any significance for us to-day?" In many respects Charles Simeon's life and times are more remote from ours than his were from the Middle Ages. We think differently, we feel differently, we speak differently, from Charles Simeon and his contemporaries. The whole structure of our society and way of life is different from theirs. Can a study of Simeon and his times be anything but a visit to a museum? To this question there are two answers—the answer of the historian and the answer of the man of religion. Let them be distinguished.

The historian, for his part, would insist that the study of history is not simply the study of the past but is also the study of how the past became the present. We may or may not come into this world "trailing clouds of glory" but we certainly do come trailing the past. If the child is the father of the man, no less certainly is the great-grandfather the great-grandfather of his own great-grandchildren, though no doubt sharing that relationship with others! And sometimes it happens that the great-grandfather within the particular setting of his own time sets certain influences to work which are still discernible in the lives of his descendants. So we believe it was with Charles Simeon and with the legacy he left to his spiritual heirs, not a few of whom are quite ignorant of the source from which they derive their inheritance.

Let a contemporary historian of the Church of England, one who has already contributed a notable study of Charles Simeon, bear his testimony. Canon Charles Smyth, writing of Simeon, gives this considered judgement:

"I doubt whether the genius of that man as an ecclesiastical statesman has ever received sufficient recognition. He seems to me to rank with Samuel Wilberforce, Bishop of Oxford—the Remodeller of the Episcopate, as Burgon calls him—as one of the founding fathers, or Remodellers of the Church of England in the nineteenth century."[1]

That century does not merely linger on into the twentieth. In all its strength and its weakness "nineteenth century" England is still moulding our affairs, certainly in the Church, and hardly less so in the State. While we may properly regret our inherited weaknesses and strive to outgrow them, we shall be wise, in Church and in State, to nourish what is strong. It is after all more than possible that Great-Grandfather will provide us with some of the necessary vitality to resist the sinister apotheosis of "Big Brother".

But whatever may prove to be the enduring contribution of the nineteenth century to the State and to Society as a whole, its contribution to the Church of to-day enshrines the workmanship of Charles Simeon, and that in three respects.

In the *first* place he safeguarded for the Church of England a pattern of devotion, in no sense definable along party lines, whereby a passionate concern for evangelism was proved to be consistent with Church Order, the while it derived much of its nourishment from the Church's liturgical life. The Church of England had already seen one tragic secession of evangelical vitality and devotion when it lost John Wesley and the Methodists. But for Charles Simeon there might well have been an even greater withdrawal half a century later. The very length of his

[1] C. H. E. Smyth, *Simeon and Church Order*, 1940, p. 6.

ministry at Holy Trinity Church, Cambridge, extending as it did
through a period of revolutionary upheaval, may well in itself
have been one of the important factors which gave time for the
tradition he represented to establish itself as wholly at home in
the Church of England.

No doubt, as Canon Smyth has also made clear, a further factor
was Simeon's highly responsible purchase of "spheres of influence". The words "highly responsible" are both just and
accurate. Simeon was concerned to ensure that there should be
available within the Church of England, *as that Church then was*,
centres where a liberating Gospel could be preached and men and
women offered a pastoral ministry based upon that Gospel. In
that day and generation it is doubtful if any alternative method of
securing that end existed. Simeon's "Trustees" were given
statesmanlike and profoundly spiritual terms of reference. It is
perhaps worthy of note that in his sermon in Holy Trinity Church,
Cambridge, on 22 November 1936, the then Archbishop of
Canterbury bore this testimony:

"No better manual for all patrons of Benefices could be found
than the Deed which declared his Trust. I am bound to add that
in my experience his trustees have been loyal to the spirit of this
Trust."

The *second* aspect of Charles Simeon's workmanship which is
still in evidence is the care and attention that he devoted to preparing men for the Ordained Ministry of the Church of England.
In his time there was for all practical purposes no special training
for the ministry afforded by the Universities; while theological
colleges, otherwise than a small one in the Isle of Man, had not
yet come into existence. Simeon's conversation parties and
lectures in his rooms in King's College, and his sermon classes,
were an attempt to meet a great need. There in his College rooms
throughout his long ministry hundreds of future clergy of the
Church of England received their only training for the ministry.
Canon Charles Smyth, in another of his books, has two comments
on this aspect of Simeon's ministry which are relevant here.

"Simeon", he writes, "was almost the first man in the history
of the English pulpit since the Middle Ages to appreciate that it
is perfectly possible to teach men how to preach, and to discover
how to do so."[1]

[1] C. H. E. Smyth, *The Art of Preaching*, 1940, p. 175.

And later, speaking of his practical effect on the English pulpit, Canon Smyth says Simeon's "insistence upon the primary importance of method in sermon construction was not wasted . . . the basic principle that the sermon ought to have an outline, and the notion that it ought normally to be divided into three parts sandwiched between an introduction and an application, persisted throughout the 19th century, and are still persistent."[1]

Those are the comments of the author writing as an historian. In the same volume the same author, as a great preacher himself, shows to the full how Simeon's evangelistic purpose permeated every sermon he preached and inspired all his instruction about preaching. His counsel in this respect is as fresh to-day as when he first gave it a hundred and fifty years ago.[2]

In the *third* place the workmanship of Charles Simeon is to be discerned in the tremendous impetus he gave to the missionary movement of the nineteenth century, and more particularly to that of the Church of England. It would indeed be wrong to exaggerate his influence to the extent of giving him an isolated prominence above that of that notable company of friends who were all as devoted as himself to this sense of world-wide mission. It was the fact of his position in the University life of Cambridge which made his influence so vast and so lasting. Simeon's influence in this respect was, in his own Cambridge, like a river which, taking up into itself many tributaries, broadens out as it moves towards the sea. No one will wish to belittle the significance of these tributaries or their contribution to the volume of the waters. But the main stream of missionary zeal, at least in the University of Cambridge, has for more than a century drawn much of its inspiration from influences which derive ultimately from that astonishing ministry of fifty-four years as a Fellow of King's College and Vicar of Holy Trinity Church.

The answer of the historian, then, would seem to be that Charles Simeon has a significance for to-day precisely because to understand who he was and what he did is one of the clues to understanding ourselves.

What answer to our question will be given by the man of religion, assuming for purposes of analysis his distinction from the historian? Has Charles Simeon anything to say which has a

[1] Smyth, op. cit., p. 208.
[2] Smyth, op. cit., pp. 176–8.

bearing upon our lives to-day? This is a more difficult question to answer because changes in the language of devotion create peculiar barriers to the full appreciation of the nature of religious experience as enjoyed in another age than one's own. Two illustrations may be taken from Charles Simeon's own words. In the first of these he is certainly speaking into our contemporary situation. Indeed his words are of enduring significance, however much the theological battle-lines may have changed. In the Preface to his *Horae Homileticae* he writes:

"The Author is no friend to systematizers in Theology. . . . He has no doubt but that there is a system in the Holy Scriptures (for truth cannot be inconsistent with itself); but he is persuaded that neither Calvinists nor Arminians are in *exclusive* possession of that system. He is disposed to think that the Scripture system, be it what it may, is of a broader and more comprehensive character than some very exact and dogmatical Theologians are inclined to allow: and that, as wheels in a complicated machine may move in opposite directions and yet subserve one common end, so may truths *apparently opposite* be perfectly reconcilable with each other, and equally subserve the purpose of God in the accomplishment of man's salvation. . . . He bitterly regrets that men will range themselves under human banners and leaders, and employ themselves in converting the inspired writers into friends and partisans of their peculiar principles. Into this fault he trusts that he has never fallen. One thing he knows, namely, that pious men, both of the Calvinistic and Arminian persuasion, approximate very nearly when they are upon their knees before God in prayer. . . . And what both these individuals are upon their knees, it is the wish of the Author to become in his writings. . . ."[1]

That could hardly be better expressed to-day when systematizers are once more very much in evidence.

It is worth noting how Simeon instinctively finds the resolution of conflict in the place of worship. In this instinctive trend of his whole personality, which found a thousand expressions in his life, Simeon is speaking home to one of the deep places in the heart of contemporary man, for all that he is, maybe, largely unconscious of the depths within himself. Unconsciousness of this dimension of depth is perhaps the gravest symptom of the sickness which is spreading like a consumption across the world to-day.

[1] Charles Simeon, *Horae Homileticae*, Vol. I (1832), Preface, pp. xxiii–xxiv.

Simeon lived deep. Life for him was adoration and death the opportunity for learning more of what adoration ought to mean. Because in any case this is tragically remote from the attitude of most of us, an expression of this in Simeon's very uncontemporary language may shed some light on the true nature of a religious man. I have in my possession, if a personal note may be allowed, three letters written by Charles Simeon to my own great-grandfather. Written in 1836, a few months before his own death, they were, as to the first two, much concerned with the proper disposition of the soul here in preparation for the life of the world to come. This is not a common contemporary preoccupation. Let Simeon then speak to those who can hear:

"It has often been said by persons, and it is with many a very favourite idea, 'I shall, at my admission into the divine presence, shout louder than anyone.' *I expect it will be far otherwise with me.* I expect rather to fall upon my face, with the deepest self-abasement, and not even to venture to lift up my eyes, until especially enjoined to do so; and then to sing only with a tremulous and scarcely audible voice, such as in some favoured seasons I have uttered in God's house below, the wonders of redeeming love. . . . I think our heavenly Bridegroom will be best pleased with that state of mind, which most accords with the real condition of our souls. . . . True He has forgiven me; but can I forgive myself? Must not every testimony of His love towards me make me hate myself ten times more, and abhor myself in dust and ashes? This then is the way in which I would go in and out before Him here; and in which I even *desire* to meet Him, when I shall come into His immediate presence *hereafter.*"

We would be unlikely to express ourselves like that to-day, but it can hardly be denied that in his recalling of us to a certain fundamental attitude of mind Charles Simeon is immensely relevant to one of the deepest needs of man not only in our own but in every age

Such then, in brief compass, is one man's estimate of the claims of Charles Simeon upon the attention of churchmen in the middle of the twentieth century. The essays which follow present the man in the setting of his time. It is because he was faithful in that setting that he has a word to speak to us to-day. In the communion of the people of the Most High we are all contemporaries.

M. A. C. WARREN

I

SIMEON IN THE SETTING OF THE EVANGELICAL REVIVAL

G. C. B. DAVIES

Simeon in the Setting of the Evangelical Revival

DURING THE nineteenth century, a strong reaction set in against the outlook and standards of the eighteenth-century Georgian Church. This reaction has extended to the present century, so that it is still customary for that time to be regarded as of little interest or importance. Such a view has been tempered by a more just appraisal of the conditions of that period in recent years; and although the main lines of criticism remain true, yet the environment and circumstances of the Church of that day can now be seen in improved perspective.

The relationship between Church and State was of considerable significance. The country had experienced the change from a dominant monarchy to party government, and the Church's influence was a highly important factor in party conflict. The long alliance between Whig ministers and Whig prelates of the first half of the century was considered necessary both to maintain the Hanoverian succession and to buttress the Establishment. Episcopal influence was strengthened by providing the assurance that the privileged position of the Church would be maintained. If the Church Whigs were the key to the situation, the Tories and many Tory Jacobites still manned scores of parishes throughout the country. This political position, together with the suppression of Convocation since 1717, was a major cause of the Church's ineffectiveness in matters spiritual.

But the Church was certainly not a neglected feature of monarchical or of governmental interest. The year 1800 marked the forty-first of the reign of George III, and a glance at Royal policy in connection with higher Church appointments reveals clear affinities with the reign of Queen Anne, so linking together the beginning and close of the century. The king valued few duties of the royal prerogative more highly than his right of nomination to the episcopal bench. While he might recommend his ministers

9

to seek out discreet and learned men for preferment, yet at times he could intervene decisively in favour of particular candidates. An outstanding example was his selection of Manners Sutton, Bishop of Norwich and Dean of Windsor, for the primacy on the death of Archbishop Moore in 1805. This he did, despite the indignant protest of Pitt who, favouring Pretyman-Tomline, Bishop of Lincoln, complained that he had not been honoured with the king's confidence in the matter as had his predecessors. This, however, was entirely in keeping with several previous royal nominations, including those of Markham to York and Beilby Porteus to Chester in 1777, and in particular with the successive appointments of Hurd to Lichfield and Coventry, and Worcester, and his nomination to Canterbury, which last Hurd declined.

But continuity of royal custom, amply reflected in the continuity of ecclesiastical practice in general, ill accorded with the changing times. For this period, which saw the blow to national prestige abroad in the Declaration of American Independence, also witnessed at home the enormous social upheaval consequent upon the beginnings of the Industrial Revolution, with its shift of population from country to town. The last quarter of the century saw the growth of mushroom cities, with the vast problems, economic, social, and religious, which attended so widespread a migration. To these new circumstances, and in particular in the matter of building new churches to meet the needs of the industrial workers, the Church was totally unable to adapt itself. The necessity for an Act of Parliament to be passed for the creation of each new parish was partly responsible for this inertia; but further cause lay in the fear, and at times the determined obstruction, of vested interests to proposed changes, together with the ingrained apprehension of "enthusiasm" characteristic of churchmen during this century. To these long-standing factors opposing all change, there was added after 1793 the powerful support of popular reaction to the excesses of the French revolutionaries, evoked by the fear of similar disturbances arising in this country. Indeed, as has been pointed out, the "unhappy generation from 1793 to 1826 contributed more than any of its predecessors to the ill-repute of the eighteenth century by its policy of repression and reaction, which, though resolute in opposing all who laid even the mildest hands upon the established order in church and state, allowed the accumulation of anomalies and abuses in such magnitude as to provoke the radical reform epoch which succeeded".[1]

English fears in face of French extravagances and rationalism were expressed in divers ways. A deeper sense of the stabilizing effect of an established Church led to an increasing reluctance to tamper with existing conditions, and an increasing respect for the continuity of Anglican tradition and practice. Parochial clergy received a new vision of their vocation as leaders of the Church militant against atheism, privy conspiracy, and rebellion. Even the worst abuses of ecclesiastical privilege or indifference were elevated to unwonted dignity when overlaid with the gracious mantle of custom and tradition. Bearing in mind the ecclesiastical and administrative reformation of the 1830s, it is difficult to visualize the climate of public opinion which had widely acclaimed the "Reflections" of Burke only some forty-five years earlier. Then he had written: "[The people of England] can see without pain or grudging, an Archbishop precede a Duke. They can see a Bishop of Durham, or a Bishop of Winchester, in possession of ten thousand pounds a year, and cannot conceive why it is in worse hands than estates to the like amount in the hands of this Earl or that Squire."[2] Within thirty years or so, the people of England saw very differently, thanks to the writer of the *Extraordinary Black Book* and other Liberal reformers.

If the episcopate of the Hanoverian Church has been summarily dismissed as composed of time-serving mediocrities, more concerned with politics than with pastoralia, yet certain exceptions should be noted which serve to qualify such a sweeping generalization. Foremost among these at the turn of the century was Beilby Porteus (1731–1808). After a brilliant career at Cambridge, he moved to Lambeth in 1762 as domestic chaplain to Archbishop Secker. In 1777 he became Bishop of Chester, as already noted, being translated to London in 1787. His life was marked throughout by a conscientious attention to his duties, and by a breadth of tolerance, and sympathy with social and pastoral problems in advance of his time. In 1778, he was among those who signed the unsuccessful petition to Archbishop Cornwallis for some reform

[1] N. Sykes, *Church and State in England in the XVIII Century*, 1934, p. 407, to which this essay is much indebted throughout.
[2] E. Burke, *Reflections on the Revolution in France*, 1790, p. 154.

of the Articles and Liturgy. As Rector of Lambeth, he had endeavoured to effect a better observance of Lent, Good Friday, and other Holy Days. He was a close friend of Hannah More, and approved of her literary work and philanthropic efforts. He was also one of the few bishops to support the newly-formed British and Foreign Bible Society, and such other activities of the Evangelicals as the Sunday school movement, the abolition of the slave trade, and the cause of foreign missions, while he worked to secure the better payment of clergy in an endeavour to mitigate the evils of pluralism and non-residence. Bishop Shute Barrington (1734–1826), of Llandaff, Salisbury, and Durham, should also be mentioned as another prelate who identified himself with earnest and progressive work wherever he found it, but if for this reason he supported the Evangelicals, he cannot be identified with their views. He maintained a friendship with Charles Daubeny, a prominent High Churchman, and patron of William Paley, and was noted for his liberal outlook. A third figure, and the outstanding scholar, was Samuel Horsley (1733–1806) of St David's, Rochester, and St Asaph. His Charges were particularly impressive in their defence of Trinitarian doctrine against Unitarianism, though even he confessed, on his translation to Rochester, that he was glad to be relieved of the costly and tiresome journey to the principality each summer. As against such representatives of episcopal activity there must be recorded the name of Richard Watson (1737–1816), Bishop of Llandaff, who openly confessed that he owed his elevation to the episcopate not to the zeal or industry with which he had for many years discharged the functions and fulfilled the duties of Professor of Divinity at Cambridge, but rather to the expectation of the Whig government that he would prove a useful supporter of their administration. Of such a scandalous appointment it need only be said that if his support and championship of the rights of Protestant dissenters to enjoy the full liberties of public life are to be warmly commended, his discharge of his duties in South Wales from the shores of Lake Windermere for the major part of his episcopate is to be as roundly condemned, even by eighteenth-century standards.

The outlook of the majority of the clergy of this period has been characterized by the adjective "latitudinarian". Originally applied in the seventeenth century to those Anglican divines who attached relatively little importance to dogmatic truth, the epithet

was equally appropriate during the Hanoverian epoch if its interpretation be extended to include a similar indifference to ecclesiastical organization and liturgical practice. Reason rather than
revelation was the "candle of the Lord", while as a natural
outcome their Arminian preferences made these clergy hostile to
the predominantly Calvinistic Methodists and Evangelicals. This
factor was primarily responsible for the prevailing dislike of
"enthusiasm", a term which came to be applied to Methodist and
Evangelical alike. Yet the rise of the Evangelical movement was
the most remarkable spiritual factor of the time. As a result of
recent research, the view long held that new life came to the
Anglican Church only through the extra-ecclesiastical efforts of
the brothers Wesley has been largely modified. Many of the foremost Evangelical clergy owed their awakening, humanly speaking, to the reading of such works as William Law's *Serious Call to
a Devout and Holy Life*, or to the influence of some outstanding
leader such as Samuel Walker of Truro in gathering together a
small body of like-minded men for further fellowship and instruction. This is in no sense to belittle the work of the great
itinerant evangelists, but only to emphasize that this movement
pursued its own course, within the Anglican Church, touching
and influenced by the Methodists, yet largely independent of them.
Beginning with small groups centred around Walker at Truro and
Venn at Huddersfield, its early adherents included such outstanding characters as Romaine (for long the only Evangelical
incumbent in London), Newton of Olney, Fletcher of Madeley,
Scott, the commentator, of Aston Sandford, Adam of Wintring-
ham,[1] Grimshaw of Haworth, and Berridge of Everton, to name
only a few. These men attracted attention by their holiness of
living, and by their emphasis on preaching the gospel of salvation
by personal committal in faith to the Christ, whose death on the
Cross had won for mankind forgiveness of sins and the opening
of the kingdom of heaven to all believers. These tenets, never
wholly forgotten, but long latent, brought to many new hope,
joy, and peace. Opposed at first by ecclesiastical authorities (of
whom Lavington at Exeter was particularly virulent) they
gradually won increasing recognition and respect for their
admirable zeal and energy, which drew crowded churches and

[1] Not "Adams" as in C. H. E. Smyth, *Simeon and Church Order*, 1940, p. 255.
This same error occurs in Carus, p. 107.

resulted in well-instructed congregations. One aspect of their teaching deserves special notice. If they were faithful in preaching the Word, they were equally faithful in administering the sacraments, and to this their communicant figures bear eloquent testimony even from the earliest days of the movement. When Grimshaw of Haworth was reported to the Archbishop of York (Hutton) in 1749 for his share in the Leeds Conference of Methodists, the Archbishop asked him: "How many communicants did you find on coming to Haworth?" "Twelve," replied Grimshaw. "How many have you now?" "In winter, between three and four hundred according to the weather. In summer sometimes nearer twelve hundred," was the answer. Whereupon the Archbishop remarked: "We can find no fault in Mr Grimshaw seeing that he is instrumental in bringing so many to the Lord's Table."[1] Wesley's *Journal* makes two references to the Haworth communicants, recording on 22 May 1757, nearly a thousand, and on 22 July 1759, "the communicants alone filled the church".

At the Northamptonshire village of Creaton, procured by Simeon in 1785 for Thomas Jones, who laboured there for nearly fifty years, we find a similar zeal in the discharge of parochial duties. For years the attendance at Holy Communion on the first Sunday of the month never fell below eighty-five, which meant that the entire adult population of the village were communicants. At Christ Church, Macclesfield, David Simpson laboured with such success that on Good Friday 1782, he had over thirteen hundred at Holy Communion. Walker stressed the importance of attending the sacrament at Truro, as did Venn at Huddersfield. Moreover, not only was most earnest attention paid to Church services and the teaching of the Bible, but these clergy exerted themselves to show that the religion of Jesus Christ was concerned with the whole range of human life and interests. Indeed, the moral improvement which can be traced in the life of England between the latter part of the eighteenth century and the 1830s was very largely due to the work of the Evangelicals, who took every opportunity to abolish cruelty in all its forms.[2] The testimony of Liddon confirms this opinion, for he wrote: "The world to come, with its boundless issues of life and death, the infinite value of the one Atonement, the regenerating, purifying, guiding

---

[1] G. G. Cragg, *Grimshaw of Haworth*, 1947, p. 56.
[2] Halévy, *England in 1815*, 1949 ed., p. 453.

14

action of God the Holy Spirit in respect of the Christian soul, were preached to our grandfathers with a force and earnestness which are beyond controversy. The deepest and most fervid religion in England during the first three decades of this (i.e. the nineteenth) century was that of the Evangelicals."[1]

If this was true of the Evangelical clergy, the lay adherents of the movement provided equally notable leaders. "A spacious mansion on the confines of the villa-cinctured common of Clapham,"[2] home of Henry Thornton, Member of Parliament and wealthy banker, became the headquarters of the group which drew to itself the name of the "Clapham Sect". Here the Thorntons, Granville Sharp, Lord Teignmouth, and, above all, William Wilberforce brought to bear upon the whole country an intense moral earnestness combined with charitable and practical philanthropy which has left a permanent mark upon the life of the Church. In countless ways, this whole group of devoted laymen forwarded the Evangelical cause. Their lives were strictly ordered. They prayed, worked, gave alms and performed their deeds of charity with scrupulous devotion, bearing in mind the solemn account which they must one day give to the Judge of all the earth. Wilberforce and many others gave three hours of the day to prayer. Thornton before he married spent six-sevenths of his income in charity and afterwards a third.[3] They read and studied the Bible with the utmost care, if uncritically, seeking for the message which they believed it brought to them individually. They observed Sunday with strictness, assembled their households for family prayers, and published the organ of the movement, *The Christian Observer*, with Zachary Macaulay as its editor, which disseminated their views to an ever-widening circle.

But the work for which they will always be remembered, upon which they were vigorously engaged at the opening of the new century, was the abolition of the slave trade. Even in 1791, William Wilberforce at thirty-two was so identified with the movement with which his name will be for ever associated, as to receive a letter from John Wesley written only a week before his death. It well expressed the evangelist's appreciation of the formidable difficulties to be surmounted:

[1] *Life of Pusey*, 1893, i, p. 255.
[2] J. Stephen, *Essays in Ecclesiastical Biography*, 1891 ed., p. 523.
[3] R. Coupland, *Wilberforce*, 1945 ed., p. 251. On the Clapham Sect, in general, cf. also M. Hennell, *John Venn and the Clapham Sect*, 1958.

"Unless the Divine power has raised you up to be an *Athanasius contra mundum*, I see not how you can go through your glorious enterprise in opposing that execrable villany, which is the scandal of religion, of England, and of human nature. Unless God has raised you up for this very thing, you will be worn out by the opposition of men and devils. But if God be for you, who can be against you? . . . Go on, in the name of God and in the power of His might, till even American slavery (the vilest thing that ever saw the sun) shall vanish away before it."[1]

Wilberforce's speech in the House of Commons of 12 May 1789 marked the opening of the great Crusade. "So much misery condensed in so little room is more than the human imagination had ever before conceived. So enormous, so dreadful, so irremediable did its wickedness appear that my own mind was completely made up for the abolition." It has been called one of the finest speeches in all that golden age of Parliamentary oratory, and it lasted for three and a half hours. Yet the speaker could record in his diary: "Came to town sadly unfit for work, but by Divine grace was enabled to make my motion so as to give satisfaction." This indeed was true, and the greatest of the orators was quick to acclaim it. "The house, the nation, and Europe," said Burke, "are under great and serious obligations to the hon. gentleman for having brought forward the subject in a manner the most masterly, impressive and eloquent."[2] But the struggle had to last for some twenty years. Thomas Clarkson, the tireless traveller and investigator, abandoned his Deacon's Orders to engage in the work. The cause suffered a serious setback by the outbreak of the French Revolution. Many were preoccupied with the greater national campaigns. The promulgation of the Declaration of the Rights of Man in Paris in 1789 led to a slave rising in St Domingo, with massacres on both sides. In England, Wilberforce's Bill was defeated in Parliament eleven times, even though in April 1792, it received the support of a magnificent oration by William Pitt. Instead the House then voted for the subtle amendment of Dundas, whose motion that "the Slave Trade ought to be *gradually* abolished" was carried by 230 votes to 85.

Great sums of English capital were involved in the trade, and many and varied were the arguments employed to maintain the

---

[1] *John Wesley's Letters*, Vol. VIII, p. 265.
[2] Coupland, op. cit., p. 102.

existing situation. The English merchants and West India planters would be ruined; there would be negro risings on the plantations, if they believed that their emancipation was in prospect; profitable trade would pass to the French. Pitt refused to make it a Government question, neither would he take steps to check the immense increase in the traffic brought about by the war. But in the end principle prevailed. The Slave Trade was made illegal by Act of Parliament on 23 February 1807. The Bill, carried by 283 votes to 16, has been described by Lecky as one of "the three or four perfectly virtuous acts recorded in the history of nations".[1] It is not overstating the case to claim that, after the high drama of the war, the abolition of the slave trade occupied the next place in the nation's attention. The campaign was not yet finished; in 1811 the trade was made a felony, but not until 1833 under the leadership of Sir Thomas Fowell Buxton, was slavery itself abolished throughout the British dominions. If many had raised their voices against the iniquities of slavery, yet the main enthusiasm, most of the money, and nearly all the labour of collecting evidence, condensing it, and disseminating it by propaganda and through appropriate pressure groups came from the Evangelicals.

Yet this was not the only cause which bore the mark of their enthusiasm, though it was certainly the most famous. The call of the unevangelized heathen, in particular of Africa and India was deeply exercising the minds of their leaders. The Society for the Propagation of the Gospel celebrated its centenary in 1801, but it was limited by its charter to work among white settlers. The Society for Promoting Christian Knowledge, founded a few years earlier, restricted itself to work at home, and in the main to an extensive area of south India. Grant had endeavoured to persuade his colleagues in the East India Company to permit missionaries to enter and work in the country among the natives. Wilberforce also had sought unsuccessfully to persuade Parliament to incorporate in their charter a clause to the effect that the Company owed a duty "to seek the religious and moral improvement of the native inhabitants". Charles Simeon was able to secure the appointment of several men as chaplains to the Company, among them Henry Martyn, whose short but invaluable ministry included the translation of the New Testament into Hindustani. A year after Martyn's death, Wilberforce secured, in 1813, the

[1] W. E. H. Lecky, *History of European Morals*, 1869, i, p. 161.

passing of a resolution not only that facilities should be given for missionary work, but that the Church in India should be placed under the superintendence of a Bishop and three Archdeacons. Missionaries, if refused a licence by the Company, could appeal to the Government. Though the Anglo-Indian body hotly opposed this provision, it was supported by Castlereagh and carried.[1]

But a more positive step had been taken. On 12 April 1799 a small body of men possessed with vision and enthusiasm, and a profound spirit of prayer, met in the Castle and Falcon Hotel, Aldersgate Street. As a result of their deep concern for the expansion of the Church, there was founded the Society for Missions to Africa and the East, afterwards known as the Church Missionary Society. The Chairman was John Venn, Rector of Clapham; Henry Thornton was treasurer, and Thomas Scott, secretary. The work of this Society, as recorded in the monumental history by Eugene Stock, has grown and prospered to an extraordinary degree, celebrating its third jubilee in 1949, thus more than fulfilling the earnest hopes of its founders. Other societies founded by the Evangelicals were the Religious Tract Society, also in 1799, and the British and Foreign Bible Society in 1804. Further societies were to follow; the London Society for promoting Christianity among the Jews (1809), a society for work in the oldest colony, Newfoundland, which grew into the Colonial and Continental Church Society (1823), and in 1836 the Church Pastoral-Aid Society to help in providing further support for the clergy of the Church at home. This is a fine record of activity, revealing the many good causes in which the Evangelicals were concerned. Nor was this all. They had a lively interest in education, and in particular in the Sunday school movement. Hannah More, by her writing of books and popular tracts, reached the poor of the village of Cheddar, where by her philanthropic and educational work she effected something of a reformation. She and her sister were warned that their lives might be in danger, but they persisted in their good work, encouraged by some of the local incumbents, and by such visitors as William Wilberforce and other well-known Evangelical leaders. For many years her tracts had a wide circulation throughout the country.

But this sketch of Evangelical work and witness, though en-

[1] Coupland, op. cit., p. 320.

couraging, has left two questions outstanding. How numerous were the Evangelicals, and wherein lay their weaknesses? The second question is easier to answer than the first. The very strength of Evangelicalism, its emphasis on the individual and personal nature of religion, was also its weakness. That true religion is personal is undeniable; but too often Evangelicals did not consider their relation to the Church, the Body of Christ, or to human society in general. Later generations have perceived this fault and worked to eradicate it, but this perception did not appear necessary at first. Though in the main loyal Churchmen, having a particular affection for the Prayer Book, there were certain questions which they were not as yet prepared to face. A contemporary criticism of their failings came from the anonymous publication, *Zeal without Innovation*, in fact written by James Bean, which appeared in 1808. After remarking that "it is a matter of fact, that our churches are not so well attended as they formerly were", the author proceeds to investigate the causes for the lack of sabbath observance, and makes the significant point that "it is observable that where our liturgy is used in its grandest form, the attendance is as far from being numerous as it is elsewhere". Even the most effective rendering of the service in the heart of London with its million inhabitants did not prove a sufficient attraction, for "with a numerous attendance of ministers, the finest specimens of church music, and these performed with that effect which professional qualification gives to such compositions, the seats at St Paul's cathedral are seldom more than half filled. The circumstances may be thought by some not to merit much consideration; but it ought to have a place in the account, as it serves to show how little hold our church, under *any* of her forms of administration, has on the minds of the people: she is passed by with equal indifference, whether she appear dressed in cathedral state, or in the plainer attire of parochial service!"[1] In face of this general neglect of church worship, it was unfortunate, in the author's opinion, that Evangelical clergy were not in all cases whole-hearted supporters of the customs and usages of the Established Church. It was held against them that they preferred the prayer meeting and the sermon to the Liturgy. "By their preaching," continues the same author, "while they revived an attention to some neglected truths of the first importance to

[1] Op. cit., pp. 1–4.

mankind, they brought on a mean opinion of the form of religion. To this, as one cause, we may perhaps ascribe the almost entire desertion of our churches on prayer days, though more to the increased disregard of all religion." A further point enumerated among "some justly censurable things found among the class of clergymen, called evangelical ministers" was the distinction which they were apt to draw between "gospel labourers" on the one hand and the main body of the clergy on the other. Among some Evangelicals, "the clergy as a body are considered . . . as men who do not preach the gospel; an imputation which, in their account, implies the forfeiture of all that reverence and support which is due to Christian instructors. Nor can it be maintained that their favourite preachers are universally innocent of being, in some degree, the cause of so ill an opinion respecting the clergy. Some of them are not content with enforcing what they believe to be necessary to salvation, and showing the evil tendency of the contrary doctrine; but mingle therewith such intimations of a general departure from the truths of the Gospel, as their hearers naturally apply to the persons really meant by the preacher to be included in the censure; that is to say, the clergy in general. . . . Of a piece with the conduct here noticed, is the language which some included in this class of clergymen use, in reference to those parishes in which their own views of Christianity are not inculcated. Of such places, though the ordinances of Christian worship be regularly administered in them, they speak in terms similar to those which the antient prophets expressed themselves, when describing the state of heathenism. Thus leading the unthinking to blend appointments ordained for the honour of the living and true God with idolatrous institutions: as if there were no difference between diminished light and absolute darkness; between sinking below the level of completely evangelical instruction, and the entire absence of Christianity."[1] The sin of the Pharisees, spiritual pride, was an ever-present danger, which might prove a pitfall for unwary ministers in their zeal for the salvation of souls, however outstanding might be their concern for what they considered to be the primary task of their ministry.

And this leads to the further question, how influential and how numerous were the Evangelicals, who at the turn of the century

[1] *Zeal without Innovation*, pp. 152–4.

could point to few dignitaries in their ranks,[1] and whose work lay entirely at the parochial level? This has been variously estimated. It has been pointed out that the assertion of Lecky that "by the close of the [eighteenth] century the Evangelical party was incontestably the most numerous and the most active body in the English Church"[2] was in fact contested by Gladstone, whose statistics clearly show that this was not the case. "If instead of the words 'party' and 'numerous', one might substitute 'influence' and 'definite' ", remarks Canon Overton, "the historian's assertion would, perhaps, be nearer the truth."[3] In fact, Lecky qualified his statement in later editions of his work: "by the close of the century the Evangelical party, though still a minority, had become a large and important section of the English Church".[4] The reasons for the vitality of the Evangelical party have been summarized as the spiritual earnestness and activity of its leaders; the admirable organization of the party; the real practical work of Christian piety and charity undertaken by its members, and the ineptitude of much of the opposition staged by their antagonists; while the very name "Evangelical" told greatly in their favour. And I can do no better than add in the words of Overton: "If it be thought that too much space has been devoted to the Evangelicals, the apology is that they constituted by far the most prominent and spiritually active party during the greater part of the period before us. They were the salt of the earth in their day and the Church owes a debt of gratitude to those holy men . . . which it will never forget so long as personal piety and the spiritual side of religion are valued at their proper worth."[5]

Amongst the leaders of this movement for over fifty years, spanning the time from the outbreak of the French Revolution to the eve of Queen Victoria's accession, few names are more honoured than that of Charles Simeon. The bicentenary of his birth provides an appropriate opportunity for a reappraisal of his contribution both to the Evangelical movement, and to the spiritual life of the Church of England as a whole. Superficially, the circumstances of his home background, of his youth and early manhood, would appear to be in few respects different

[1] The Hon. and Rev. Henry Ryder only became Bishop of Gloucester in 1815.
[2] *History of England in the Eighteenth Century*, ii, p. 620.
[3] J. H. Overton, *The Evangelical Revival in the Eighteenth Century*, 1900, p. 158.
[4] Lecky, *History of England in the Eighteenth Century*, 1892 ed., iii, p. 126.
[5] J. H. Overton, *The English Church in the Nineteenth Century*, 1894, pp. 108f.

from that of many other young clergymen of his time, while apart from the tumultuous early years of his incumbency at Trinity Church, Cambridge, the last fifty years of his life were singularly lacking in incident. Yet behind this apparently uneventful existence, there lay an influence and authority of incalculable benefit and power not only in the university, but far beyond its walls. Charles Simeon was born at Reading on 24 September 1759, a year which also saw the birth of William Pitt the younger and of William Wilberforce. Charles's father, Richard Simeon, an attorney, was the son and grandson of successive Vicars of Bucklebury in Berkshire. His mother, Elizabeth Hutton, came from a family which had given two archbishops to the see of York. Charles was her fourth child, but she died before he was old enough to have many memories of her. Of the other children, Richard, the eldest, died young in 1782; the second, John, became a Fellow of All Souls', a Master in Chancery, one of the Managers of the private property of George III, and Member of Parliament for Reading. He was created a baronet in 1815. The third, Edward, was one of the Directors of the Bank of England, a successful and wealthy merchant, who died in the prime of life after receiving faithful and devoted help from his younger brother.

Charles was sent to Eton at the age of seven, and it is possible from various sources to obtain a fairly accurate picture of him in his schooldays. Apparently he possessed unusual strength and agility, for in a letter of his friend, Dr Goodall, later Provost of Eton, written in 1833, we read: "I much doubt if you could *now* snuff a candle with your feet, or jump over half a dozen chairs in succession."[1] Known as "Chin Simeon", he was extremely ugly as a small boy, and therefore sought compensation by exercising a taste for extravagant dress. Richard Porson, indeed, later the Cambridge classical scholar, wrote some crude rhymes addressed "to the ugliest boy in Dr Davies' dominions", but though Simeon made every effort to trace the author, even comparing the handwriting with that of other boys in his form, he was deceived by the author's use of the left hand.[2] Simeon also had the reputation of being a good judge of horseflesh. Riding was his favourite exercise, a pastime which he en-

[1] Carus, p. 3.
[2] C. H. E. Smyth, *Simeon and Church Order*, 1940, p. 47, to which this section is indebted.

joyed throughout his life. Intellectually he was not remarkable while at school, though he was always ambitious to acquire distinction in some way. Looking back, as his biographer is at pains to stress, from the matured outlook of middle life, Simeon regarded his youth as almost wholly unprofitable. "I begin then with *my early life.*—But what an awful scene does that present to my view! Never have I reviewed it for thirty-four years past, nor even can I to my dying hour, without the deepest shame and sorrow. My vanity, my folly, my wickedness, God alone knoweth, or can bear to know. To enter into a detail of particulars would answer no good end. If I be found at last a prodigal restored to his Father's house, God will in no ordinary measure be glorified in me: the abundance of my sinfulness will display in most affecting colours the superabundance of his grace."[1] It is with this stern self-criticism in mind that the biographer proceeds to quote a letter written in 1782 by Henry Venn to a friend, declaring of Simeon: "This is the young man who was bred at Eton College; so profligate a place, that he told me he should be tempted to murder even his own son (that was his word) sooner than let him see there what he had seen."[2] Further light upon the lack of religious instruction at Eton appears in a letter written some years later by Simeon to Goodall. "It is often with me a matter of regret that the atmosphere of Eton is so unfavourable for the health of the soul; and that amidst all the attention that is paid to the Poets and Philosophers of Greece and Rome, scarcely ever by any chance is the name of our blessed Saviour heard, especially in a way of admiration and love; and that whilst earthly honours are held up as proper objects of our ambition, so little is spoken of heaven as worthy of our pursuit."[3] Yet it is probable that Eton was not so conspicuous in its reputation as Simeon might seem to imply, for contemporary references to other public schools of the period make equally vigorous complaints of the lack of instruction in the Christian religion, and of low moral standards. One school experience was recalled by Simeon in later years. He had been much impressed at the idea of the whole nation being called to fast and pray on a particular day during the American War of Independence. Conscious of his own sinfulness, he spent the whole day in fasting and prayer, only to incur the ridicule of his companions, who quickly dispersed his good

[1] Carus, p. 4. [2] Carus, p. 27. [3] Carus, pp. 609f.

desires. But he was thought by his school contemporaries to be particularly strict and devout.

The incident that changed his whole life occurred almost as soon as he came up as an undergraduate to King's College, Cambridge, in 1779. On the third day after his arrival, the Provost informed him that at mid-term, the Holy Communion was to be administered in the chapel, and he must communicate on that day. His own record of the occasion is given in the *Memoir*. "What! said I, *must* I attend? On being informed that I *must*, the thought rushed into my mind that Satan himself was as fit to attend as I; and that if I must attend, I must *prepare* for my attendance there. Without a moment's loss of time, I bought the old *Whole Duty of Man* (the only religious book that I had ever heard of) and began to read it with great diligence; at the same time calling my ways to remembrance, and crying to God for mercy; and so earnest was I in these exercises, that within the three weeks I made myself quite ill with reading, fasting, and prayer.... The first book which I got to instruct me in reference to the Lord's Supper (for I knew that on Easter Sunday I must receive it again) was Kettlewell on the Sacrament; but I remember that it required more of me than I could bear, and therefore I procured Bishop Wilson on the Lord's Supper, which seemed to be more moderate in its requirements.... My distress of mind continued for about three months, and well might it have continued for years, since my sins were more in number than the hairs of my head... but God in infinite condescension began at last to smile upon me, and to give me a hope of acceptance with him.... But in Easter Week, as I was reading Bishop Wilson on the Lord's Supper, I met with an expression to this effect: 'That the Jews knew what they did when they transferred their sin to the head of their offering.' The thought rushed into my mind, What! may I transfer all my guilt to another? Has God provided an offering for me, that I may lay my sins on his head? then, God willing, I will not bear them on my own soul one moment longer. Accordingly I sought to lay my sins upon the sacred head of Jesus; and on the Wednesday began to have a hope of mercy; on the Thursday that hope increased; on the Friday and Saturday it became more strong; and on the Sunday morning (Easter-day, April 4) I awoke early with those words upon my heart and lips, 'Jesus Christ is risen today; Hallelujah! Hallelujah!' From that hour peace flowed in rich abundance into my soul; and at the Lord's table in our chapel I had the sweetest access to God through my blessed Saviour."[1]

The memory of this experience frequently returned to him during succeeding years, leaving him in no doubt but that God had wrought a work of grace in his soul. On his arrival home for the long vacation, he began the custom of family prayers morning and evening for the servants, and to his great delight his eldest brother, Richard, joined them. Thereafter his progress in the spiritual life was evident, if not without fluctuations. He was ordained deacon by Bishop Yorke of Ely on Trinity Sunday, 26 May 1782, though still an undergraduate (he did not take his B.A. degree until January 1783), his Fellowship at King's being accepted as a title. He began his ministry in St Edward's Church ("in good old Latimer's pulpit"[2]) taking duty for the Vicar, Christopher Atkinson, during the long vacation. An important result of this connection was his introduction to John Venn, who soon took him to see his father, Henry Venn, Rector of Yelling, some fifteen miles from Cambridge. So commenced a friendship with both father and son which proved a decisive influence upon the life of the young clergyman, bringing him much necessary wisdom and balance, and saving him from the many pitfalls of inexperience and over-enthusiasm.[3]

In October 1782 Richard Simeon died, and it was thought desirable that Charles should leave Cambridge and live with his aged father. Everything was settled, and he was within a fortnight of departure when the death occurred of Henry Therond, incumbent of Trinity Church. For some time Simeon had marked the position and size of this church, with the wistful hope that one day it might be given to him, "but as to the actual possession of it, I had no more prospect of attaining it, than of being exalted to the See of Canterbury".[4] But now Simeon requested his father to move Bishop Yorke to secure his appointment. This was done, though not without opposition from the parishioners, who favoured the appointment of the afternoon lecturer, the Reverend John Hammond, and petitioned the bishop for him to be made incumbent instead. The bishop, however, was not to be coerced, and made Simeon a firm offer of the living. This he accepted, preaching his first sermon on 10 November 1782. He soon learnt

[1] Carus, pp. 6–9.　　　　　　　　　　[2] Carus, p. 21.
[3] See Smyth, op. cit., ch. 6.　　　　　[4] Carus, p. 41.

what it meant to be known as an Evangelical. The seat-holders deserted the church, locking the doors of their pews that no one should use them. When Simeon placed forms in the aisles, the churchwardens threw them out into the churchyard, and for over ten years of his ministry, his congregation had to stand. Undergraduates came in large numbers, bent on breaking up the services. "For many years", wrote one of his contemporaries, Henry Gunning, "Trinity Church and the streets leading to it were the scenes of the most disgraceful tumults. In vain did Simeon . . . exert himself to preserve order in the church; in vain did Professor Farish,[1] who as Moderator was well-known and popular with the undergraduates . . . station himself at the outside door to prevent improper conduct to the persons leaving the church; and though one undergraduate, who had been apprehended by Simeon, was compelled to read a public apology in the church, the disturbances still continued."[2] But Simeon persisted with quiet perseverance, not doing anything deliberately to provoke opposition, but not yielding to the temptation to preach only an acceptable message. Gradually he won toleration and at length recognition as the most powerful religious force in Cambridge. His work in training undergraduates for the ministry, through Bible study and sermon classes, in days before theological colleges existed, was of particular importance. His support of missionary work and the formation of a Trust to purchase advowsons so as to secure continuity of Evangelical teaching, were other factors in his far-sighted policy. But perhaps his chief strength and most lasting influence lay in his insistence upon an ordered and disciplined ministry; in refusing to be drawn into irregularities, and by scrupulous care in maintaining the rules of order of the Church. His wisdom and statesmanship saved many enthusiastic young men from drifting into the ranks of non-conformity, so assisting to maintain Evangelicalism within the Church of England at a most formative period of its development. For this above all his memory deserves to be had in honour, as the character of this Evangelical leader is recalled to those who minister in the mid-twentieth century. With him, heart and mind were united in service of incalculable value and outstanding faithfulness to the Church in Cambridge, in England, and indeed throughout the world.

[1] Tutor of Magdalene College, and Vicar of St Giles.
[2] H. Gunning, *Reminiscences of Cambridge*, ii, p. 138.

2

SIMEON AND THE BIBLE

ROBERT S. DELL

Simeon and the Bible

CHARLES SIMEON often used to say: "The Bible first, the Prayer Book next, and all other books and doings in subordination to both."[1] There is no doubt that he himself placed the Bible first as his authority in theological and ethical matters, and turned to it continually as the source of inspiration for his devotional life. He made a life-time study of it, with the aim, not only of becoming acquainted with its teaching, but of living by its principles, and making known to others, in all its fullness, the Bible view of life as he understood it. His loyalty to Scripture is reflected in every aspect of his career—in his personal life, in his public ministry, especially in his preaching, in his published works, in his contribution to the wider work of the Church through helping to found Societies, and encouraging men to go overseas as Chaplains and Missionaries, and in the work which was perhaps nearest to his heart, namely, his dealings with successive generations of Cambridge gownsmen as their spiritual adviser and senior Christian friend. In fact, it was the depth of his grasp of Biblical doctrine, combined with the sanity of its application, which made his influence so extensive and lasting.

Following his spiritual awakening during his first term at King's College, Simeon soon acquired the habit of regular Bible study, which became the main interest and activity of his working life. In the early morning, when most Cambridge dons were still in bed, he was hard at work, studying the Holy Scriptures, and meditating upon them in such a way that their truths sank into the depths of his personality, and moulded him into the mature Christian character he became. Having no family responsibilities, freed from domestic cares in his College Fellowship, without teaching duties, and living in an age when parochial work made less demand upon the time of the clergy, he had ample time to devote to this study. Time, like money, was for him a sacred trust from God, for which he must one day give strict and solemn

[1] Brown, p. 12.

account; there was never, therefore, any inclination on his part to waste it. This study was the foundation of his public ministry of over fifty years' duration at Trinity Church, and the inspiration and refreshment he drew daily from the Bible made him an effective agent in the awakening of both town and gown, neither of them previously touched by the rising tide of religious revival associated with the names of Wesley and Whitefield. Simeon did not merely read Holy Scripture as men read other books. "We must search in them", he said, "for hid treasures, and lay up in our hearts, yea in our inmost souls the glorious truths which they unfold to our view."[1] His study, as his sermons attest, was a diligent search for this treasure hidden within the sacred text. "What enemies to their own souls they are", he exclaimed, "who neglect the Holy Scriptures."[2] "Let us examine them with deep attention", he urged in another sermon, "as we would a will or testament by which our title to a large inheritance was to be determined."[3] So we gain the impression of a man in deadly earnest, with all the intensity of his vigorous nature, searching the pages of Holy Scripture for the truth, which, like the Kingdom of Heaven in the parables of Christ, is reserved for those who seek for it. Nor was it at all surprising that Simeon, a churchman of the later eighteenth century, should turn so resolutely to the Bible, for there was in England a long tradition of Biblical theology, stretching from Wyclif and the Lollards, through the Reformation and seventeenth-century divines, to Wesley and his fellow-Methodists. The young Simeon, however, was a convinced churchman, uninfluenced by Methodism. As Wesley's course was drawing to its close, he was laying foundations by his study of the Bible at Cambridge, for a life which was to help secure a recognized place within the Established Church for an Evangelical Movement, to be nurtured and built up in the Protestant Biblical tradition.

Yet the circumstances of his religious awakening combined with his independent frame of mind to make him extremely wary of all religious parties and human systems of theological thought. He saw how easily men impose their own views upon Scripture, and interpret it according to their own fancies. "As for names

---

[1] Sermon 203—"The Scriptures Recommended to Us."
[2] Sermon 1054—"The Word of God Precious."
[3] Sermon 975—"The Means of our Justification before God."

and parties in religion he equally disclaims them all: he takes his religion from the Bible and endeavours as much as possible, to speak as that speaks."[1] "If in anything he grounded his sentiments upon human authority, it would not be upon the dogmas of Calvin or Arminius, but on the Articles and Homilies of the Church of England."[2] His reason for so doing was not submission to an official creed, but because he found the truths they stated in "the sacred Oracles". "The author", he wrote in the preface to *Horae Homileticae*, his twenty-one volumes of sermon-outlines, "is no friend to systematizers in Theology. He has endeavoured to obtain from the Scriptures alone his view of religion; and to them it is his wish to adhere, with scrupulous fidelity; never wresting any portion of the Word of God to favour a particular opinion, but giving to every part of it that sense, which it seems to him to have been designed by its great Author to convey."[3] He did not expect, therefore, to find favour either with Calvinists or Arminians, since they were bound to find teaching inconsistent with their theories in what he had written, but he concluded that Scripture itself was not, apparently, thoroughly consistent in a logical way, and was satisfied with his own inconsistencies so long as they were those of Scripture itself. "He has no doubt that there is a system in the Holy Scriptures (for truth cannot be inconsistent with itself); but he is persuaded that neither Calvinists nor Arminians are in exclusive possession of that system. He is disposed to think that the Scripture system, be it what it may, is of a broader and more comprehensive character than some very exact and dogmatic Theologians are inclined to allow: and that, as wheels in a complicated machine, may move in opposite directions and yet subserve one common end, so may truths apparently opposite be perfectly reconcilable with each other, and equally subserve the purposes of God in the accomplishment of man's salvation."[4] Instead of trying to reconcile, for example, the truth that a man may do nothing without God's help with its apparent opposite, that God expects a man to exert himself in the service of the Kingdom, he is content to accept both truths and hold them in tension. A man might lapse into sloth if he thought personal effort was not required of him; he might boast of his achievements if he thought personal effort

---

[1] Preface to *Horae Homileticae*, p. xiv. [2] Op. cit., p. xiv, note e.
[3] Op. cit., p. xxiii. [4] Op. cit., p. xxiii.

31

alone could accomplish Divine purposes. Scripture is balanced and provides warnings in both directions for those that need them. Or again, we can believe at the same time in the holiness of God and in the existence of sin, though if God is omnipotent and hates sin it may be logically inconsistent to do so. In Simeon's day there were those who held, on the one hand, a rigid doctrine of Divine Election and Predestination, while others stressed, on the other hand, the fact that God loved and called *all* men, and that they, having the power of free will, were capable of responding to him. Simeon accepted both positions in so far as he found them both in Scripture. Instead of attempting to find a mean between extremes, he held both extremes at once. He used to say: "When two opposite principles are each clearly contained in the Bible, truth does not lie in taking what is called the golden mean, but in steadily adopting both extremes, and, as a pendulum, oscillating, but not vacillating between the two."[1] In an unpublished letter to Miss Evans of Darley, Derbyshire, he deals with this point. "If I were asked", he wrote, "Are you a Calvinist? I should answer, No—Are you an Arminian?—No. What then are you? I should answer, A Bible Christian. All that God says in his word, I say, without embarrassment and without fear: and on whichever side of the Post the inspired writers run, I run after them: and if any tell me, 'You are wrong', I reply, 'Tell Paul so, and Peter so, for I am misled by them': and if they press me further with my inconsistencies, I send them to my watchmaker, to shew him the folly of putting his wheels in opposite directions, by which they must of necessity knock one another to pieces. (If the watchmaker tell him, that the wheels have cogs, by means of which, instead of breaking each other to pieces, they concur to the production of one common end, peradventure he may learn something there, which he did not choose to learn from me.) If he do not choose to learn from so poor a Mechanic, I send him to the great Mechanic who formed the Universe, to ask him, how it is that he has continued to make the heavenly bodies move so regularly in their orbits? I shrewdly suspect that, when he is told, that all those orbs have in the first place received an impulse which would have driven them to an infinite distance from each other in wild confusion to all eternity, but that at the same time they were all made to feel an attractive influence from the great

[1] Brown, pp. 74-5.

centre of their system, the sun, and that by the inward influence of both they are kept in a due Medium, I say, when I have referred him to this great exemplar, he may be disposed to become a Bible Christian too. Proud Man is fond of human wisdom: the Bible Christian is a fool. The one is wise and becomes a fool: the other is content to 'become a fool, that he may be wise'."[1] It is interesting to see Simeon taking arguments which were familiar to people of his own age, and using them to support his own characteristic position. The famous argument of Paley, the proof of God's existence from design, was based on the analogy of the watch, which must have been made by someone: similarly, the contemplation of the Universe led one to the conclusion, that it had a Divine Architect and Creator. Simeon's watch mechanism, however, illustrated to him his own favourite theme, that apparent contradictions in Scripture were working towards a common end. The planets moving in their orbits did not tell him, as they told Addison, that they were made by a divine hand; they told him rather that there was an overruling purpose in God, which controlled the seeming chaos of opposing forces. These arguments of Simeon's were aimed at producing convinced Bible Christians, i.e., people who were prepared to take the Bible at its face value and follow its teaching wherever it led them. Another illustration he used was intended, perhaps, to catch the attention of the games player rather than the astronomer, engineer, or mechanic. "That ball lies in the middle of the table," he said. "I wish to propel it straight forward, but at the same time to act by two opposite powers on the right hand and on the left, either of which singly would propel the ball away from the straight line. I combine both, and they propel it in the way I wish."[2] He seems to say that there is an order in the plain unsophisticated following of Scripture, which arises from the interplay of apparently opposing forces. It cannot be neatly tied up and labelled in the manner possible with systems of thought of human origin. It is larger than any such system, which is not surprising, since it is the truth of God. Taken in its entirety it produces a balance and a precision not possessed by other systems. Its very breadth may cause criticism from those who confine themselves to well tried theological positions, but it does, in fact, preserve men from the dangers which appear to accompany most human systems of

[1] Simeon's Trust Papers.　　　　[2] Brown, p. 268.

theological thought. Simeon certainly believed it to be the case. "I keep simply to Scripture and not to system", he said, "and nobody quite likes me. Like a man swimming in the middle of the Atlantic, I am not afraid of striking my feet against sunken rocks, I am in no danger of running against either America or Africa."[1] Simeon's contention was that there is danger in any attempt to build up a body of dogmatic theology, unless it is as wide and comprehensive as the Bible itself. "God has not revealed his truth in a system: the Bible has no system as such. Lay aside system and fly to the Bible; receive its words with simple submission, and without an eye to any system. Be Bible Christians, and not system Christians."[2] It would probably be true to say then, that Simeon by his influence upon generations of ordinands at Cambridge, founded a new school of Biblical thought in the Church of England. Taught by him, they abandoned the Calvinism of the earlier Evangelical Churchmen; warned by him they avoided the Arminianism of the Wesleys. They were to be Bible Christians, and seek as far as possible to be loyal to the whole revelation of Scripture. So Preston in his *Memoranda of Simeon* writing in 1840 is able to say that "the Scriptural in contra-distinction to the systematic mode . . . is gaining ground in the Church".[3]

But it may well be asked how anyone can be loyal to the teaching of the whole of Scripture, since every student must seek to interpret the meaning of what he reads, and all exposition is liable to error. Whilst many have held, as Simeon did, the authority of the Bible as the word of God, the one rule of faith and practice, no sensible man could believe in the inerrancy of his own understanding of Scripture. Simeon was well aware of this difficulty. "My endeavour", he said, "is to bring out of Scripture what is there, and not to thrust in what I think might be there."[4] In his preface to his published sermon-outlines, he declared it his intention to show "how texts may be treated in a natural manner".[5] "He has endeavoured, without prejudice or partiality, to give to every text its just meaning, its natural bearing, and its legitimate use."[6] In other words he took a text in its whole context, and sought to expound its meaning. This method may be seen carefully worked out in the volumes of his sermons. He there

[1] Op. cit., p. 132.   [2] Op. cit., p. 269.
[3] M. M. Preston, *Memoranda of the Revd. Charles Simeon*, 1840, p. 30.
[4] Carus, p. 703 (2nd ed.).   [5] Preface to *Horae Homileticae*, p. vi.
[6] Op. cit., p. xxvii.

contrasted the method he followed with that adopted by others. Of the "Scottish Systematizers", for example, he said: "Perhaps they view texts in general too much as isolated authorities, and not sufficiently in reference to their contexts."[1] He sounded a warning against building up theological systems upon isolated words in Scripture. "I avoid building on words only. The Methodists rest much on St Paul's expression, 'A second benefit' (2 Cor. 1.15) as a second new birth, a coming of age; whereas the whole context shows it means no such thing; but merely pointed to establishing the Christians by preaching a second time. The Moravians take hold of the word 'Token' (Ps. 86.17) and ask every one, 'Have you got your token for good yet?' All such modes of speaking as this are very foolish, and is trifling with Scripture, and building a sect or system upon strained interpretations of single words."[2] It was not that Simeon rejected the authority of single words or underestimated their importance. Indeed, few divines of the period weighed the Scriptures as carefully as he did, seeking to give due weight to every word. His protest was against the misuse of words, torn out of their context, to be used as a basis for human speculation, however well intended. Of the importance he attached to even single words, we have evidence in many of his sermons. "God will not allow us to suppress or add one single word,"[3] he once said. He found Scripture perfect "as a revelation from God", and "as a directory to us".[4]

In a letter to Bishop Burgess he explained a little more fully how he set about the task of exposition. "My mode of interpreting Scripture is this. I bring to it no predilections whatever: for though I have in my mind the analogy of faith, and am aware that no portion of the Scripture, rightly interpreted, can contradict that, yet I never wish to find any particular truth in any particular passage. I am willing that every part of God's blessed Word should speak exactly what it was intended to speak, without adding a single iota to it, or taking from it the smallest particle of its legitimate import. If there be a doubt which a candid mind would feel. I readily state that doubt, and leave it to have its full operation against what I conceive to be the juster interpretation."[5]

---

[1] Brown, p. 135.   [2] Op. cit., p. 234.
[3] Sermon 2535—"The Perfection and Sanctity of the Holy Scriptures."
[4] Ibid.   [5] Carus, p. 540.

In all his attempted exposition of Scripture, Simeon was aware of the frailty of human reason, which by itself could not fathom aright the meaning of "God's oracles". In fact, he taught that the reader needed the enlightenment which only the Holy Spirit could give; and he illustrated it in this way. "If we look at a sundial, we may understand the use and import of the figures; yet can we not attain a knowledge of the time unless the sun shine upon it. So it is with respect to the Word of God."[1] Thus, in the Simeon tradition, prayer for illumination is linked with the reading of the Scriptures, and there is reliance upon the Holy Spirit to lead the believer into all truth. "Scripture read in the spirit of prayer teaches practical wisdom; but read in another spirit, only enlightens the understanding, and not always that."[2] Not that anyone could ever attain to the perfection of truth in all its aspects. "There is in all the words of Scripture a depth which we cannot fathom."[3] It should be clear then from all that has been said on the subject that Simeon was a most careful and conscientious expositor of Scripture. Within the limits of the knowledge of his age, and starting from his premises concerning the Bible, he worked out a full Biblical doctrine of the great Christian themes. He was not an independent thinker, nor would he have wanted to be, since his avowed intention was to think again the thoughts of the Apostles and Prophets, apply them to his own soul and life, and pass them on to others to do the same.

Bishop Wilson, writing of Simeon after his death, said of him that "as a Preacher, he was unquestionably one of the first of his age—as a Divine, one of the most truly Scriptural".[4] It was his aim in preaching to take as great a variety of texts as possible for public exposition. "Ministers in general", he said, "take too confined a range of texts and subjects. We should preach more widely, and bring Scripture truths forward in all subjects on which they properly bear. There would be a larger and better body of divinity abroad were Ministers to do so."[5] He followed by precept what he urged upon the young gownsmen, who gathered so eagerly in his rooms in the Gibbs building in King's week by week, to learn from his accumulation of wisdom, divine and human. He set

---

[1] Sermon 975—"The Means of our Justification before God."
[2] Brown, pp. 166–7.
[3] Sermon 1448—"The Resurrection proved."
[4] Carus, p. 847.   [5] Brown, p. 254.

himself to preach on all the books of the Bible, and from such a wide variety of texts that his twenty-one volumes of sermons form almost a commentary upon the whole Bible. There are altogether 2,536 sermons, each having a different text, 1,277 drawn from the Old Testament, and 1,259 from the New Testament.

It is not surprising to find among the sermons a number devoted to the subject of the Scriptures themselves. In preaching, for example, on Jeremiah 15, verse 16, a sermon entitled "The Word of God Precious"[1] he makes three points about the Word of God and its reception by men: it is necessary for all; it is suitable for all; and it is sufficient for all. He speaks also of the effect it will produce in men, and ends by reflecting what enemies to their own souls they are who neglect the Holy Scriptures, and what an unspeakable blessing is the Bible Society. He urges his hearers in many passages to read the Bible privately for themselves. Its ultimate design is to render men perfect, but this cannot be accomplished without a desire to know God's will combined with a readiness to perform it. He saw that in the world generally the Scriptures produced little effect, because men were not in touch with God through Christ, and had therefore no desire for the kind of life offered to them there. "The Bible is a sealed book to unbelievers . . . but let them once experience a taste of the Redeemer's love and instantly they will find in the inspired volumes mines of wealth."[2] It is faith, not learning, which is required for a right understanding of the Scriptures and of the Christian life, faith in the Christ whom these Scriptures reveal, and to whom that life is lived. Many simple people have had this faith with little knowledge of the Bible, but there is no doubt that faith is enriched by the kind of fare the Bible provides, and where it has been available for their use, Scripture has developed the spiritual understanding of even the simplest and most unsophisticated people. But in Simeon's day, as in our own, there were many people who had less time and talent to devote to the study of the Bible than he himself had. This problem was brought to his attention, and his solution of it is an interesting foreshadowing of a method very widely used to-day by a great many people in every land who belong to the various Scripture reading unions and associations. "It will be said by many, that their memory is defective, and that they cannot retain the things which

[1] Sermon 1054.   [2] Sermon 880—"The Wells of Salvation."

37

they read or hear: but if we made a practice of selecting daily some short portion of Scripture for our meditation throughout the day, the most ignorant amongst us would soon attain a knowledge which at present appears far beyond our reach."[1] But Simeon saw that if people were to read the Bible for themselves and make it their own in this way, there must be a far greater supply of Bibles available for their use. This need was not limited to the United Kingdom, but extended to people of other races and cultures. Hence his advocacy of the Bible Society and its work of translating the Scriptures into the world's many languages, printing, and circulating it at the smallest possible cost to the purchasers. So the saintly Henry Martyn, Simeon's disciple and curate for a while at Trinity, devoted his brilliant talents as a scholar to the work of translating the Scriptures into the Persian language. This was pioneer work undertaken at great sacrifice by a few devoted men. There can be no doubt, however, that the growing activities of this Society, together with its sister Societies in many lands, has made the Bible the world's best seller, and brought its message to millions, who might not otherwise have heard it. The revival of Biblical theology in recent times within both the Protestant and Roman Catholic Churches is one of the signs of hope in a despairing generation, and owes much, not only to the dedicated work of scholars, but also to the patient work of translation and distribution undertaken by the Bible Societies. In all this the pioneers of the Society would no doubt rejoice, and, not least amongst them, Charles Simeon.

His style of preaching differed very considerably from that of his contemporaries, mainly because there was in him an urgency which sprang from his apostolic faith and zeal. His delivery was earnest and forceful, compelling the attention of his hearers in a way that the discourses of Latitudinarian clergymen were not calculated to do. Many of the sermons of the age would have consisted in expositions of the wonders of the created order as proofs of the rationality of belief in God, or of moral lectures upholding the ideal of duty. Emotion of any kind was excluded as bad form in polite society, and religious "enthusiasm" was regarded with horror by members of the Established Church. Simeon's matter as well as his manner was altogether different from the formal sermons of others. Those who heard him

[1] Sermon 2187—"Love to the Scriptures Recommended."

preach—and as the years went by crowds flocked to Trinity Church, week by week, and to Great St Mary's, the University Church, when Simeon was to preach the Sermon—saw a man, utterly convinced by the truth which he was proclaiming, setting forth with all his energy the doctrines he found in the Bible, and enshrined in the Prayer Book and formularies of the Church of England. They saw there not a fanatic, but a man of education, not an open-air preacher of the Lollard or Wesleyan type, but one who had spent his whole life in his college in Cambridge, yet a man convinced by what he taught and convincing in the style in which he proclaimed it. Behind his public ministry lay hours of patient study and hard work. His advice to young preachers is still worthy of consideration by all would-be preachers. "Let him get his text into him in his study, and then get into his text in the Pulpit."[1] Such preaching can never be dull! He believed in driving home the points of his sermon as hard as possible, so that his hearers had no doubt of his meaning, and of what response was required of them. This was impressed upon his mind by a simple illustration: "I met with this expression lately in a Pastoral charge—'screwing the word of truth into the hearers'. It is strange, but powerful. The screw is the most powerful of mechanical forces. The screw, as it turns round and round again and again, is forced deeper and deeper, and gains such a hold, that it is impossible to withdraw it by force from the wood in which it is inserted. So with the truth you would teach your hearers . . . in my sermons the application is always another turn of the screw, and where I can, the very hymn which I select for the singing is a turn of the screw."[2] Such preaching is likely to be effective in every age, especially when it is backed by a forceful and dedicated personality. One thing which Simeon thought to be new in his age was the use made of the Bible as "a converting Book" as opposed to "an establishing book".[3] It was his emphasis upon two great doctrines which he found prominent in Scripture, namely, atonement through the Cross of Christ, and justification by faith, both of which he preached to induce personal response in his hearers, that made his ministry a powerful influence in the conversion of many to a full acceptance of the Christian Faith.

Yet great preacher as he was, he was delighted when he came across a poor old woman, living on the Trumpington Road, who,

---

[1] Brown, p. 180.   [2] Op. cit., p. 197.   [3] Op. cit., p. 149.

though she "loved to hear Mr Simeon preach", enjoyed even more something which " 'the other gentleman, the gentleman in white used to read every service'. 'I think they called it the Lesson', she said. 'Those lessons did me a great deal of good and comforted me.' 'What a testimony', remarked Mr Simeon, 'to the power of Scripture does this old woman's saying afford'."[1] Like all great preachers he realized what was the source of his power, namely, that the truth, which was being proclaimed, captured the attention of the hearers more than the manner in which it was preached, and above all that it was the Holy Spirit mediating Christ to the people through his Word. The preacher was only a faithful herald, proclaiming the good news as a servant of Christ, the Word of God.

Simeon's method of expounding Scripture saved him from those absurd excesses which have often marred the extremer advocates of narrow Biblical systems. His strong faith and devotional approach to Scripture preserved him from regarding the Bible merely as a set of proof-texts in an argument or as a source-book of theological definitions, whilst his sanctified common-sense and essential sanity kept him from going beyond the revelation he found and building up fanciful theories. He kept in view always the primary purpose for which revelation was given—"Scripture (is) given to make men wise unto salvation— not to make them wise as God is wise".[2] He warned the young men of his Cambridge circle against excessive zeal in matters which did not arise from the teaching of the Bible. There is always a tendency for immature Christians to attempt to go beyond the Christian standard to some form of asceticism, and warnings similar to those given by Simeon need to be sounded to every generation of young religious zealots, warnings to which, unfortunately, they are seldom inclined to listen! Simeon was able to say, however, that "one of the great blessings of a Cambridge education is that here we lose our rigidity: as stones on the sea-shore lose their angles by rough friction so do we. Love, and collision with others soon rub off our asperity of doctrine".[3] The kind of thing with which Simeon had to contend was, of course, different from the problems faced by a College Dean to-day. His

---

[1] Op. cit., p. 153.
[2] M. M. Preston, *Memoranda of The Revd. Charles Simeon*, 1840, p. 26.
[3] Brown, pp. 280–1.

approach to the matter may be illustrated by a comment, for example, on Ecclesiastes 7, verses 16, 17—"Be not righteous overmuch". "Religion is the regulation of our lives by God's holy word", he said. "If we propose a rule not laid down by God, we give religion as it were an undue weight in our minds; we are righteous overmuch. All superstition is of this kind and its tendency is not to save us, but to destroy."[1] He warned his readers in the Preface to *Horae Homileticae* also against "so perverting the Scripture as to make it refer to Christ and his salvation, when no such object appears to have been in the contemplation of the inspired writer".[2] These people he hesitatingly calls "ultra-Evangelical". In their exposition of Scripture they overlook in many passages the practical lessons taught, and detect only the leading *doctrines* of the Gospel. When they speak of "the Gospel" they mean it in the narrow sense of their own definition—e.g., salvation through the atoning sacrifice of Christ. In the minds of some adherents of this position to-day every sermon should be "evangelistic", i.e., should proclaim "the Gospel" so that men may be converted to Christ. The result of such preaching is often to produce men and women hardened against the appeal of Christ and the Cross. Simeon avoided this error since he gave a due consideration in his preaching to the lessons of morality, which, in their place, he held to be as useful and important as the doctrines of grace. He recommended his published sermons to those "who prefer the plain and obvious comments of sobriety to the far-fetched suggestions of a licentious fancy".[3] The purpose here, as so often in what he said or wrote, was that people should search the Scriptures for themselves, and find there the balance which Simeon himself found. Unfortunately, as Protestants well know, the doctrine of private judgement, which leaves to the individual the responsibility of deciding for himself from the Bible what God teaches and requires, has led to fantastic and absurd excesses, quite as erroneous as anything ever taught by the unreformed churches. A good deal of human misery has been caused, unintentionally no doubt, by these perversions of truth, thought by their promoters to be drawn from the Bible. Evangelicals cannot evade some share of guilt in this matter. There is an interesting passage in Abner Brown's Introduction to his *Recollections of the*

[1] Op. cit., p. 170.
[2] Preface to *Horae Homileticae*, p. xxv.   [3] Ibid.

Conversation Parties of The Revd. Charles Simeon, a book from which numerous quotations have been made in this chapter. Brown, who was up at Queens' College, attended Simeon's parties from January 1827 to June 1830 and made careful notes of all he heard. He was later Vicar of Gretton, Northants, and Honorary Canon of Peterborough. He says, "Excessive spirituality—the error and snare of the Puritans of one age, the mystics of another, the Cathari of one still earlier, and of Ascetics and Eremites up to almost primitive times—was making in the minds of a good many people mere inward feelings and opinions to be everything. It was snapping asunder the links which connect man as God's servant, while on earth with that earth where God has placed him; was shrinking from God's works as polluted instead of sanctifying them by a hallowed use; and was treating as valueless the outward visible signs of the sacraments, and reading of Scripture, the very form of prayer which the Lord himself taught us,—the creeds and public symbols of sound doctrine. . . . Even the light of common sense and of honest truth seemed at times clouded in religious people. Thus, within the writer's knowledge, a devotedly pious lady, now dead, wife of a laborious and excellent clergyman, was wont to speak of the beauties of natural scenery as having on them the stamp of the wicked one. When her fine manly boys came home for their holidays, she would not allow them to stand at the windows of their father's Parsonage without making them turn their backs so as not to look at the romantic views by which the house was encircled, lest the loveliness of 'Satan's earth' should alienate their affections from the better world to come." In the same passages he speaks of the condemnation by some Evangelicals of such innocent pastimes as a taste for pictures, enjoyment of gardens, and love of poetry and music. This "Excessive idolatry of the internal and spiritual, with its corresponding contempt for everything external in regard to religion"[1] was also responsible for creating such a low view of Sacraments that clergymen administered Baptism without water, and in other ways showed their contempt of Church Order, even wishing to omit Creeds, Prayers, and Lessons in favour of the sermon, which was thought by them to be all-important. Brown wrote from the standpoint of 1862, and much had happened in the Church since Simeon's death in 1836. Yet Simeon would certainly have agreed with him,

[1] Brown, pp. 79–80.

since, as we have seen, he was essentially sane in his outlook, and as Canon Smyth has forcefully pointed out in *Simeon and Church Order* he was both loyal to the Church of England himself and laboured to make others conform to her Order. By his attitude and influence he saved the Evangelicals from being driven into Dissent.

It is a matter for speculation whether Simeon, had he lived in another age, would have accepted uncritically the view of Scriptural inspiration, which to him was inseparable from faith. There is no doubt, however, that the student of to-day is greatly helped in his understanding and exposition of many passages and texts of the Bible by a right use of the vast researches of modern scholarship. One feels that the man who wrote, "if there be a doubt which a candid mind would feel, I readily state that doubt", would never have joined the ranks of those who, frightened of the possible results of Biblical criticism, fell back on the method, condemned by Simeon in controversies of his own day, of abusing those who engaged in this work, and calling them by opprobrious names. That phase of Evangelicalism is mercifully now passing, as it is being realized more and more that the aim of all Biblical criticism is to do the very thing Simeon was trying to do, though he had perforce to work with a spade whilst the modern scholar may use a mechanical navvy. "My endeavour", he wrote, "is to bring out of Scripture what is there and not to thrust in what I think might be there."[1] His method of trying to do this remains valid in our own day and is indeed the only sound way—the careful exegesis of words and passages in their context. If his words had been heeded some modern heresies, built up as they are upon particular parts of the Bible to the exclusion of the rest, might have been avoided. The "Second blessing" Simeon specifically mentioned, and much modern holiness teaching has included the idea. The eschatological teaching of the Bible has been taken by some and exalted into an all-embracing theology. Others have taken particular parts of the truth, such as the doctrine of the Atonement, and applied to it the name "the Gospel" as though it were the whole Gospel. The attempt to create new systems of theology and impose them upon the Bible seems to recur continually. It will usually be found upon examination that these systems are built upon certain proof-texts, which

[1] Carus, p. 703 (2nd ed.).

have been taken like stones and built with the mortar of fallible human wisdom into a theological structure, which, however imposing it may appear, will not stand, because it is not founded on the Rock of Christ.

In speaking of Simeon's view of the inspiration of the Bible it ought not to be assumed that he was a pedantic literalist. He realized that Scripture was written in human words, which, in themselves, were inadequate to convey the full meaning which their divine subject demanded. "Scripture is written popularly, as men speak . . . it speaks of the back parts of God, His eye, His ear. It described God as mourning, grieving, repenting, laughing, etc. These forms of expression make Scripture fit for man's capacity, and enable carnal minds to obtain some view of spiritual matters. No error in doctrine or other important matter is allowed; yet there are inexactnesses in reference to philosophical and scientific matters, because of its popular style; but the precise force of a common word is not so importantly, so definitely given, as to make it the bulwark of an argument."[1] In treating Hebrews 6.4-6, for example, he saw no need to believe that repentance was ever impossible, since "Scripture often uses stronger language than will admit of literal interpretation".[2] He cites the saying of our Lord about a camel going through a needle's eye to show that Scripture cannot always be understood literally. This must be read alongside the passage quoted above, "God will not allow us to suppress or add one single word". He is willing to admit inexactness in the Bible in matters of secondary importance, in incidental references to philosophy and science, yet in matters of faith he holds clearly that it teaches without error the ultimate truth about life. Scripture provides broad general rules, the application of which to particular circumstances is part of the duty of a Christian. Notice, however, that when the Bible speaks clearly and unequivocally, the Christian duty according to Simeon's teaching is submission—"fly to the Bible, receive its words with simple submission".[3] Protestant theology at its best has taught obedience to the authority of God through the Bible, as clearly as Catholic theology teaches submission to the hierarchy of the Church. There is no idea of "do as you please" or "as you think best" in Simeon, though the place of private judgement is preserved. In the end, however, Simeon would have agreed that it

[1] Brown, pp. 99-100.   [2] Op. cit., p. 105.   [3] Op. cit., p. 269.

is the Bible which judges its readers, not its readers the Bible. In essence, he holds to the teaching of the Reformers, Luther and Calvin, and avoids that later teaching which distorted the Reformers' Biblicism into an unreasoning literalism which, ending in fanaticism, is finally destructive of true religion. The authority of the Bible for the Reformers was in Christ, the Word of God. He is mediated to the believer through the words of Scripture by the Holy Ghost. When we obey the Bible and "receive its word with simple submission", it is Christ we seek to obey. This is at the heart of Simeon's attitude to the Bible—this is the standard of faith by which he interprets Scripture; this is the faith to which he refers when he says that "he is aware that no portion of Scripture, rightly interpreted can contradict that". He approached the Bible, seeking to understand the mind of Christ, and seeking to obey the Word of God as revealed to him in its pages.

It has become clear from the numerous quotations given that Simeon accepted wholeheartedly the inspiration of the Bible, in the way that belief had been held through the Christian centuries. He speaks of them as the "Oracles of God", the "Word of God", and refers often to the "Inspired Writers". "Inspiration in my opinion, was of two kinds, according to necessity, yet ever sufficient to preserve truth:— plenary inspiration, to reveal those things which man could not know, or which the writer did not know: supervisory inspiration, to watch over the things which the writer did know and to prevent him from going wrong. God did not change a writer's character: if of poetic genius, his writing was poetic; if prosaic and plain, such also was his writing. Nay, perhaps some things might be allowed in the writer which are like error: thus, one would give one order of minute events, and another give another, for this is the fact as we see it. But whenever anything depended on chronological arrangement, then there will be found a perfect agreement." And a little further on he says, "The truths and facts of Scripture are of full inspiration",[1] or again he says that Paul "wrote by the inspiration of the Spirit of God: he also made his interpretations and alterations by that unerring Guide. It could not be accidental, for the subject is too important".[2] No other authority is of the same value for him— "We may find it useful to know something of the Fathers, and the acts of Councils, when reasoning with Papists; though even then

[1] Brown, p. 369.   [2] Op. cit., p. 283.

the thing may be carried too far. Better draw your main arguments from the infallible Bible . . . the Holy Spirit has given us one standard of all—that is Scripture."[1] The Scriptures "were indeed written by men; but men were only the agents and instruments that God made use of: they wrote only what God by His Spirit dictated to them: so that, in reality, the whole Scripture was as much written by the finger of God, as the laws were, which He inscribed on two tables of stone, and delivered to His servant Moses".[2] This is what would be called verbal inspiration or even fundamentalism in the theological jargon of to-day. In Simeon's day it was the accepted view of Scripture, and to most people would have caused no difficulty. The great intellectual movements of the nineteenth century had not then brought theology into conflict with the scientific and humanistic philosophies which have made such an impact upon Christian thinking in modern times. Natural sciences had not then presented men with altern- ative accounts than those of Genesis concerning the origin of the human race, nor had geology demonstrated the immense age of the earth. The methods of literary criticism had not in Simeon's day been applied to the Bible. One cannot but wonder what Simeon's reaction would have been to the new situation in which the Church now finds herself. One thing seems certain from his character as we know it, that he would not have acted like the ostrich which buries its head in the sand to avoid danger. He would have faced the implications of new knowledge. One small indication of this may be found in his acceptance of the findings of Dr Turton, a Cambridge Professor, who demonstrated that 1 John 5, verse 7, was an interpolation.[3] Simeon accepted this mild textual criticism. The main point, however, is that Simeon's faith, despite his language about the Bible, rested upon Christ, not upon Scripture as such. It was the fact that he found Christ in the Scriptures and that Christ spoke through them, which made him value them so highly. The Christian of to-day may be wholly at one with him in this without accepting uncritically his view of inspiration, and without attempting to close his mind to the fruits of sound scholarship or modern knowledge. One is tempted to think that Simeon, had he lived in this century, would perhaps have gloried in holding together the two extremes in this theo-

[1] Op. cit., pp. 296–7.   [2] Sermon 2133—"The Christian's Sword."
[3] See Brown, p. 355. For a fuller account of this matter, see below, p. 58.

logical debate, as he did in the argument of opposing schools of thought in his own day. He would have held firmly to the Word of God in Scripture; of that we may be sure. Would he not at the same time have weighed with care and prayer every legitimate examination of the Scripture, believing that there was yet more light to be found there? Speculation is perhaps unprofitable, but what is certain is that those who still glory in the Evangelical doctrines of their forefathers must seek in this generation to dedicate their minds to God as well as their hearts. Indeed there are encouraging signs that this is happening within the Evangelical school. Such men will be more truly in the Simeon tradition than those who attempt to impose upon the Church a doctrine of infallibility, which she has never in history accepted, without generous use of allegory as a way of escape from the impasse thus created.

Simeon's study of the Bible made him a "holy" man in the best sense of that often misunderstood word. It was not that he was without failings as he would have been the first to recognize. He had idiosyncrasies like most men of his type; he was sometimes impatient or even short-tempered. But he wrestled with himself, and by the grace of God sought to amend his life, and frame and fashion it on the Apostolic pattern and teaching. The power which so worked in him is available to-day through the same Holy Spirit upon whom he relied. The Bible which so powerfully worked in moulding and directing his life is again challenging the present generation. Perhaps we have greater difficulties, living as we do in a world in which the patterns of thought in society are no longer Christian, and in which vast new fields of knowledge are opening up—knowledge which must be employed to make interpretation relevant and satisfying. Yet the Bible remains the authoritative revelation of Christ, the source of all Christian inspiration, the guide to the One Way of Life. As we are reminded of the great things God was able to do through one life dedicated to him, we should be driven afresh to our knees to submit ourselves more fully to the Incarnate Word, the Lord Jesus Christ, who so greatly used his servant, Charles Simeon.

3

SIMEON'S DOCTRINE OF GOD

RONALD REEVE

Simeon's Doctrine of God

I

IN THE Elihu speeches in the book of Job it is suggested that the trouble with many people is that they have never asked life's most important question, Where is God my Maker?[1] Simeon, taking the question as a subject for a sermon, recorded his own answer and provided, at the same time, an excellent statement from which to begin our enquiry.

"In investigating so deep a mystery as that of what is generally called the doctrine of the Trinity, we ought beyond all doubt to look for clear and solid ground whereon to found our judgement and happily there is ample proof, throughout the whole Scriptures that though there is but one God, there is in the Godhead, a distinction of Persons, who are severally revealed to us as possessing all the attributes of Deity. The Father, the Son, and the Holy Spirit, are represented as concurring in the great work of Redemption; the Father sending His Son into the world; the Son laying down His life for us; and the Holy Spirit proceeding from the Father and the Son, to apply that redemption to our souls; and this distinction is especially recognized by every one that is received into the Christian Church; every one being, by the express command of Christ Himself, baptized in the name of the Father, and of the Son, and of the Holy Ghost."[2]

Here all of the facets of Simeon's position are displayed to perfection. We are referred to the Scriptures as being the ground of belief in God, as well as the most complete revelation of the nature of God. The historical revelation in Jesus Christ is understood as the focal point of that belief, but it is nevertheless seen in a clear trinitarian light. And this leads, not to philosophical speculation on the attributes of the deity, but to a demonstration of man's need for redemption and his opportunity to participate in it through the sacrament of Holy Baptism. Thus we see at the outset that Simeon's starting-point was the proclamation of an

[1] Job 35.10.   [2] Sermon 487—"The Impiety and Folly of Mankind."

essentially apostolic and unspeculative doctrine of God, expressed in terms of a dynamic Holy Trinity, and related at every point to the doctrine of redemption.

In company with all orthodox Christians, Simeon believed in the ultimate unity of the Godhead, claiming that it is not only repeatedly affirmed in Scripture, but is also capable of being deduced from reason.

"There is One Supreme Being, who alone is self-existent, and from whom all other beings, whether in heaven or earth, derive their existence. He, and he only, is God."[1]

Nevertheless, the argument advanced at every stage of church history against the doctrine of the Trinity, that it destroys this concept of the ultimate unity of God, is not to be admitted.

"We deny, as strongly as the Jews themselves, a plurality of Gods, and maintain, as Moses . . . asserted, 'The Lord our God is one Lord'. . . . If we so separated these Persons as to make their actions independent of each other, then we should indeed do what the Jews are ready to impute to us, worship three Gods. But we acknowledge and maintain *the unity* of the Godhead as much as they."[2]

Here then, the unity of the Godhead is seen in the συμφωνία of the divine will, especially as it is revealed in the act of redemption in Christ and his Spirit.

We are not "to conceive of the Godhead as consisting of persons of unequal majesty and glory; for the Father, Son, and Holy Ghost, are in glory equal, and in majesty co-eternal. But each person in the ever-blessed Trinity sustains a distinct office in the economy of redemption; the Father sending the Son to work redemption for us; and the Son sending the Holy Spirit to apply that redemption to us. It is in their official character alone that this subordination consists; and agreeably to this distinction, we must go to the Father, through the Son and by the Spirit; and expect blessings from the Father in the very channel by which we gain access to him".[3]

With this statement we come to Simeon's main interest under the heading of the doctrine of God. Whilst Father, Son, and Holy Spirit are One, and are therefore concerned in every divine

[1] Sermon 2465—"The Doctrine of the Trinity Vindicated."
[2] Sermon 1449—"Love to God, the Great Commandment."
[3] Sermon 2071—"The Spirit of Adoption."

activity, each has a proper function within the work of redemption. These functions of Creator, Redeemer, and Sanctifier, and the revelation of the nature of God which goes with each, make up the sum total of our knowledge of God, and therefore the only way to a full knowledge of the Trinitarian God is to know each Person in his fullness. In other words, Simeon, unlike many of his successors, could never be accused of preaching a "Christ"-religion. While his preaching was, as one would expect it to be, Christocentric, he taught a fully developed and balanced doctrine of God, Father, Son, and Holy Spirit, and would not allow either the Father or the Spirit to be overshadowed by the preaching of Christ and his Atonement. Indeed, as we now see, he insisted that the adequacy of our doctrine of God is in exact proportion to the degree in which we have personally experienced the presence and power of each Person of the Godhead in our own lives. His words may sound quaint to some, and possibly even naïve, but their trinitarian richness has not always been heard in the pulpits of the Church of England.

"How astonishing are our obligations to each person in the Sacred Trinity! The Father is the great source and fountain of all our blessings: Christ is the procurer of them, and the medium through whom they come: and the Holy Spirit is the agent, by whom they are conveyed to us. Let us hold fellowship with each in his distinct office and character, and acknowledge with gratitude their united exertions."[1]

This phrase, "Let us hold fellowship with each", is the key to Simeon's doctrine of God, for it is also the key to the historical development of the doctrine of the Holy Trinity. Theological definition must always lag behind religious experience, as Dr H. E. W. Turner has reminded us when he says, "The Church's experience of Redemption through Christ was far richer than its attempted formulations of this experience. The *lex orandi* was here, as always, prior to the *lex credendi*".[2] If this is true, then it follows that the Church's understanding of the God who wrought redemption comes primarily through the experience of being redeemed by him. This is experiential theology, which is prior to dogmatic theology, and it was Simeon's main concern. The worship and prayer of the Church has always been trinitarian

---

[1] Sermon 2002—"The Different Operations of the Holy Spirit."
[2] H. E. W. Turner, *The Patristic Doctrine of Redemption*, 1952, p. 13.

while her theology of that experience of God has proceeded more slowly from unitarian, through binitarian, to trinitarian fullness in a late, and at times hesitant, emergence. For this reason, Simeon's approach was worthy of note, for he regarded it as axiomatic that the necessary prerequisite for a living faith in the Trinitarian God is the actual experience of having been led by the Spirit to Christ and having been reconciled to the Father in the process. Such a person has actually experienced "the grace of the Lord Jesus Christ, the love of God and the fellowship of the Holy Spirit", and therefore has within himself the proof of the existence of the Triune God. He has, in fact, "held fellowship with each in his distinct office and character, and acknowledges with gratitude their united exertions", thus arriving at the catholic and apostolic doctrine of God in the same way that the Church, of which he is now a member, reached it.

While therefore it is as true to-day as it was in the time of Simeon that there are many who find themselves committed to a trinitarian formula which they cannot understand, the reason for their perplexity would appear to be that they are trying to believe the catholic articles of faith without the prerequisite evangelical experience. They cannot understand God because they do not experience him, and this explains the need that there was for the Evangelical, as for every other Revival throughout the Christian era, as the work of the Holy Spirit bringing his people back to this truth; and further it explains the continuing need for "evangelical" and "catholic" in the Church of God to-day. For it becomes increasingly obvious to those who have eyes to see, that only a "Catholic" can be "evangelical", and only an "Evangelical" can be "catholic". Perhaps it was the first glimmering of this truth in the mind of one of Simeon's several biographers, who wrote about him in the middle of the Anglo-Catholic reaction, which made him say that if Simeon had lived then (in 1863), "it is far from improbable that he would have become, without wish or effort on his own part, the leader of a very large middle party, not based upon what are called broad Church principles, but on a simply scriptural avoiding alike of the extreme Church party and the extreme Evangelical party".[1]

It has often been noted that the need for a dynamic Trinitarianism to-day is seen most clearly in our modern lack of an adequate

[1] Brown, p. 65.

doctrine of the Holy Spirit. Many twentieth-century theologians, among them Archbishop William Temple, have lamented that while the Church proclaims a firm belief in the Blessed and Undivided Trinity, the Holy Spirit still remains a *mysterium tremendi*. Nevertheless we should not allow these judgements to blind us to the truth pointed out by Dr Wheeler Robinson when he said that these post-Reformation centuries of biblical theology do, in fact, contain " 'the Arian controversy' of the Holy Spirit".[1] In other words, while the doctrine of the Holy Spirit has been relegated to, and confused with, the doctrine of the Church by Roman theologians, and has undoubtedly been neglected by some Protestant communions in ignorance of their "Reformed" heritage, it still remains a fact of Church history that it was given its due place by the Puritans, the Baptists, the Anglican Evangelicals, and the Methodists; and among these Simeon takes an honoured place with Richard Baxter, George Fox, John Bunyan, and John Wesley. As the Report presented to the Archbishop of Canterbury entitled *The Fulness of Christ* pointed out, "Both 'catholicism' and 'protestantism' allow some place for the element of personal experience, and the Reformation began, as all revivals of vital religion begin, with a renewed emphasis on experienced salvation as against contemporary formalism and arid dogmatism. Protestantism stressed the *testimonium internum Spiritus Sancti* as the normal corollary of justification by faith, thus re-emphasizing an essential element of New Testament teaching. It is a truth which can never be neglected without damming up spiritual vitality and destroying a dynamic power of true Christian living".[2] For Simeon this was a subject of grave concern to which he gave voice on many occasions, for it seemed to him that this unwillingness on the part of the majority of the members of the Established Church to accept the doctrine of the Person and Work of the Holy Spirit in its scriptural fullness could be traced to the fear of unbridled "enthusiasm" on the part of the hierarchy, and to incipient rationalism and latitudinarianism on the part of the laity. But since the Scriptures nowhere suggest that man is naturally able to obey the moral law, but everywhere speak only of a

---

[1] *The Christian Experience of the Holy Spirit*, 1928, p. 259.
[2] *The Fulness of Christ*, The Church's Growth into Catholicity, being a Report presented to His Grace the Archbishop of Canterbury by a group of Anglican Evangelicals, 1950, p. 43.

supernatural ability which is the work of the Spirit of Holiness in redeemed sinners, Simeon roundly attacked the many who "moralized" rather than preached the Gospel.

"I say, then, that without a distinct knowledge of the moral law we can have no just sentiments respecting . . . the Holy Spirit and his operations. The less is required of us, the less there is for him to do within us. And hence it is, that many deny the necessity of his influences altogether, either for the illumination of our minds, or the sanctification of our souls. The truth is that the whole denial of the doctrine of the Trinity, and of all the doctrines dependent on it—the doctrine of the atonement, of imputed righteousness, and of divine influences—must be traced to this source. Men feel not their need of a *Divine* Saviour; they feel not the need of an *Almighty* Agent, to work in them the whole work of God. Hence their principles of theology are brought down to the low standard of the Pelagian, Arian, and Socinian hypotheses."[1]

Here then we come to the crux of the matter. "Where *is* God my Maker?" We may look for him by way of the *via negativa*, but we shall only be able to say when we have done, using the words of yet another text from Job, "Lo, these are but the outskirts of his ways: and how small a whisper do we hear of him."[2] However, if we approach him as sinners in need of a Saviour, we shall find him in the fullness of his love and power, for it is in this context only that he has issued the gracious invitation, "Come unto me". To put it more technically, once we accept the Biblical estimate of man, at once we are in a position to accept also the Biblical revelation of God; and for Simeon that Biblical estimate of man was expressed in purely Augustinian terms.

"Man, at his first creation, was made in the Divine image; God communed with him as a friend, and dwelt in him as a temple; but this harmony was not of long continuance: man sinned; and God in righteous judgement departed from him. Not willing, however, that his apostate creatures should irrecoverably perish, God sent his Son to make atonement for their sins, and his Spirit to renew their natures, that so they might be restored to his favour and rendered meet for the inheritance they had forfeited."[3]

Man is only properly evaluated when he is recognized as a

[1] Sermon 2063—"The Uses of the Law."   [2] Job 26.14.R.V.
[3] Sermon 1862—"The Spirit of Christ Necessary."

sinner, whether his sin is understood in the sense of *vitium* or *reatus*. And once this conviction is accepted (which, in itself, is the initiating work of the Holy Spirit)[1] then the God who is revealed in the plan of redemption which necessarily follows, must be accepted also; *and accepted, moreover, in the way in which he has chosen to make his revelation*. So Simeon continued his argument:

"But when God had revealed a way of salvation for man through the mediation of his only-begotten Son, and through the operation of his blessed Spirit, man, though he could not *comprehend* such a mystery, must say at once, 'This, if true, is worthy of God, and fully adequate to the necessities of man': and the more deeply he considered it, the more fully would the conviction flash upon his mind. He would say, 'I can never atone for one sin; but here is a sufficient atonement for the sins of the whole world. I can never work out a righteousness wherein to appear before God; but here, in the obedience of my incarnate God, I see a perfect righteousness clothed in which I may stand before God without spot or blemish. I can never restore to my soul that likeness to God, in which it was at first created; but the Holy Spirit, the Third Person in the ever-blessed Trinity, is able to effect it, and to transform me into the Divine image in righteousness and true holiness. I see then, that supposing this revelation to be from God, there is in the salvation there proposed, a suitableness, and a sufficiency that commends it to my judgement, and must for ever endear it to my soul.' "[2]

Simeon thus came down on the side of revelation experienced in personal redemption as the only possible way in which finite man may meet and know his Infinite maker.

"We know nothing of God except from revelation. It is presumptuous, therefore, either to form notions about him from our own vague conjectures, or to refuse our assent to the representations which he has given us of himself. That there is a Trinity of Persons in the Godhead is doubtless an incomprehensible mystery: but it is plainly revealed in numberless passages of scripture ... and so clearly is it intimated in the very words of our text, that the ancients were wont to say, 'Go to Jordan, and there learn the doctrine of the Trinity.' "[3]

Here we may note before proceeding that Simeon was by no

---

[1] St John 16.8.   [2] Sermon 1532—"Judging What is Right."
[3] Sermon 1484, on the text St Luke 3.21-22—"The Baptism of our Lord."

means uncritical in his exegesis of Scripture, ignorantly claiming that the fullness of a later Trinitarian dogma could be found within the pages of the New Testament. He clearly understood that his text on the occasion of the sermon above quoted contained an implicit or incipient trinitarianism, which was to lead finally to the explicit formula of catholic belief. In this regard it is interesting to note that he was also well aware of the doubtful value of 1 John 5.7 in the Authorized Version from which he preached: "For there are three that bear record in heaven, the Father, the Word, and the Holy Ghost: and these three are one." At one of his "conversation parties" for undergraduates in his rooms at King's College, Cambridge, he spoke of the contemporary controversy between Bishop Burgess of Salisbury and Dr Turton of Cambridge, respecting the authenticity of this passage, the former urging its acceptance and the latter arguing against it. Simeon presented the evidence for both views and concluded, with the Cambridge don, that the verse was an interpolation, further pointing out that even if it were authentic, it could not be accepted as a proof-text for the doctrine of the Trinity on exegetical grounds.[1] Ultimately, he would have said, the proof of the Trinitarian nature of God rests on the authenticity of the acts of God in history; and this is only another way of saying that theology is the formulation of religious experience into universally acceptable propositions. We may, therefore, only have a doctrine of God if we know him for ourselves; and if we find him to be Father, Son, and Holy Spirit, then we must accept him as we find him, whether we may explain him or not. Hence Simeon concluded, and he was not side-stepping the problem involved:

"We are not to be sitting in judgement on God's Word and saying, I cannot understand how there should be three persons in the Godhead; or how the Son should become incarnate; or how the Holy Spirit should dwell in the heart of a believer; or how we should ultimately be saved by a righteousness not our own. I say we are not called to sit in judgement upon these things, but to receive them on the authority of God himself, who alone knows the manner of his own subsistence, or what is the mode of imparting salvation which is most suited to his own divine character."[2]

We are now in a position to sum up Simeon's statement of the

[1] Brown, p. 355.   [2] Sermon 729—"God's Word Magnified."

doctrine of God, which he does for us himself in three basic propositions which form the headings to the various parts of a sermon entitled, "The Doctrine of the Trinity Vindicated".[1]

"1. There is but one God;
2. Though there is only one God, yet there are three distinct Persons in the Godhead;
3. Each of these Persons is God, without any difference or inequality."

Beyond this statement, he made no serious attempt to define what he meant by the personality of God, merely commenting under the second proposition:

"In reference to this subject, we use the term *persons*, because there is no other so suitable: but we mean not that these persons are *in all respects* as distinct from each other as Peter, James, and John; but only that *in some respects* they are distinguished from each other, though they subsist together in one undivided essence."[2]

The main respect in which he considered them to be distinguishable from each other is in the manward activity of redemption. As seen from man's point of view, God has revealed himself in the three distinct activities of creating, redeeming, and regenerating. While these activities all have the one purpose of bringing to birth in man the *imago Dei* through creation, redemption, and re-creation, and thereby display a unity of will which confirms belief in the eternal Unity of the Godhead; nevertheless, they are also to be accepted as an indication of God's eternal Trinitarian nature. It is, of course, always tempting to over-simplify the problem of the Unity of the Godhead by regarding the distinct offices of the Father, the Son, and the Spirit in the economy of redemption as being merely temporary "modes" or "phases" of the divine activity, but this leads inevitably to the heresy of Sabellianism, and the warning must be sounded, What God hath put asunder, let no man join together. For Simeon, the conviction that the unity of will and purpose declared in the Incarnation and Pentecost could only emanate from One God was never allowed to obliterate this truth. For him it remained true that God has revealed himself to man through the experience of being reconciled to the Father through the redemptive work of his Son, and

---

[1] Sermon 2465.   [2] Ibid.

the re-creative work of his Holy Spirit. In this respect, therefore, it is vital to preserve the distinctness of the Persons in the God-head, not at the expense of the unity, but in order to establish it *in accordance with the actual, historical revelation.*

In expounding this view of the manward dispensation of God, we find in Simeon what might be called an extension of the doc-trine of the procession of the Spirit from the Father and the Son. In the Incarnation "we see the Father, *to* whom we are to draw nigh, together with the Son, *through* whom, and the Spirit, *by* whom, we are to approach him. These are evidently distinct, though subsisting in one undivided essence. Moreover the offices of the Three Persons in the Trinity are so appropriate, that we cannot speak of them otherwise than they are here declared: we cannot say, that, through the Spirit, and by the Father, we have access to Christ; or that through the Father, and by Christ, we have access to the Spirit: this would be to confound what the Scripture keeps perfectly distinct. The Father is the Original Fountain of the Deity: Christ is the Mediator, through whom we approach him: and the Spirit is the Agent, by whom we are enabled to approach him. That each of these divine Persons is God, is as plainly revealed, as that there is a God: and yet we are sure that there is but *one* God".[1]

Here we see that Simeon thought of the Son as proceeding from the Father, and the Spirit from the Father and the Son together; this being the obverse of religious experience in which the work of the Holy Spirit is to lead us to Christ, and the work of Christ is to reconcile us to the Father.

It is true, of course, that this view of the historical revelation is derived from the doctrine of the procession of the Holy Spirit *in aeternum* which, in turn, was derived from the terminology used in the Fourth Gospel in reference to the Spirit's temporal mission in the economy of redemption.[2] How far we are able to deduce the eternal nature of God from his acts in time and space is, of course, a point for considerable discussion, and it was a point which Simeon did not discuss at any length on the grounds that if God has revealed himself as being other than he really is, then are we of all men most miserable. For this reason, it would seem unreasonable to regard the doctrine of the Spirit's procession as

[1] Sermon 2101—"Access to God by the Priesthood."
[2] St John 15.26.

a mere theological fiction deduced from the Johannine use of ἐκπορεύομαι in recording the teaching of our Lord. Rather should it be accepted as the only possible explanation of the way in which the threefold revelation of God was made to man and to which the Holy Bible, taken as a whole, bears record. There is a true subordinationism within the Godhead in regard to the work of salvation, the Son being subordinate to the Father, and the Spirit to the Father and the Son together. But provided that this is understood as relating only to the act of redemption and to the work of God in relation to his creatures, and not to his essential nature *in aeternum*, there is little risk of formal heresy. It is a revealed distinction determined in the counsels of God himself as the way by which his creatures should become sons by adoption, and as such is vitally important for our understanding of the nature of God in relation to us which is, after all, the only relation we can know.

To rest content with such a basic statement of the unity in Trinity would be regarded by many, no doubt, as a mere pandering to the intellectual inability of the "not many wise, the not many mighty, the foolish and the weak", who may not pass beyond the essentially simple revelation of the Gospel to a perfect contemplation of the Godhead in the rarefied atmosphere of metaphysical speculation. Perhaps such a criticism is justified; but it also ignores the vast majority of mankind to whom God comes in redeeming love in such a way that they may understand and respond to him; and while Simeon would doubtless have agreed that there is a place for Christian philosophy, he also knew that it was not his place to supply it. His work was "to diffuse the knowledge of Christ with all the wonders of Redeeming Love", and his efforts were certainly not in vain. Although he was a Fellow of King's, it would be a mistake to think of him as a don. His lifework was not the dissemination of academic theology, but the teaching and preaching ministry of a parish priest who served the people of Holy Trinity, Cambridge, for fifty-four years. He appears to have had a natural preference for the unlearned of his parish, and although his ministry was attended by many members of the University, on whom he was to have the influence of a one-man theological college, he rarely appealed to their erudition, except in the privacy of his "sermon-parties". His primary concern was to maintain the need for personal, first-hand experience of God, Father, Son, and Holy Spirit. This, after all, is the one great experience which is offered to every man in Christ, and is the fact of God in history which Christian theology seeks to express adequately. It is not, therefore, to be despised as an unworthy contribution to our understanding of the doctrine of God, but should be accepted as a valid reminder that theology must never be relegated to the level of an academic "science of God". Doubtless, every University should have its Charles Simeon.

II

In this brief examination of Simeon's presentation of the doctrine of the Triune God, it is apparent that his emphasis was placed on the God of revelation, and not on a discussion of the nature of God *in esse*. Now, in order to prepare the way for the following essay with its discussion of his presentation of the doctrine of salvation, it is necessary to look more closely at his understanding of the economy of redemption. The act of God in Christ must ever be the focal point, for in his Person God and man are perfectly united. But coupled with the Incarnation of the Word of God is the act of God in Holy Spirit at Pentecost and beyond. If it is necessary to regard the crucifixion and the resurrection as inseparable facts of history, it is even more necessary to understand both of them in relation to the coming of the Holy Spirit. In him the new life which was revealed in Christ is made available to his faithful people; and therefore the work of the Son and the Spirit must be seen as equally inseparable.

This is evident in the first place from the fact that while we must depend on the observed work of the Son and the Spirit in the Incarnation and in the Church for our knowledge of them, it is also obvious that man's relationship with them began from the moment of his creation. Thus the re-creation of sinful man made possible through Christ, and effected in him by the Holy Spirit, is to be seen as the *new* creation because it is directly parallel with the original or old creation. The Word and the Spirit of God are seen at work in both Covenants, for both are the revelation of the same God. In Genesis[1] the *ruach Jahweh* joins with the *dabar Jahweh* as the creative power. In the Fourth Gospel, the Word who was in the beginning with God becomes flesh and is joined

[1] 1.2–3, 6, 9, 14, 20, 24, 26.

with that "other Comforter", the Holy Spirit; and together they bring about the new birth through forgiveness and reconciliation.[1] The New Covenant is new because in it a new creation comes into being by a second concerted act of the Word and the Spirit of God. Of this Simeon frequently speaks.

"The world was created by God, according to his own sovereign will, without the intervention of human aid; and, though brought into existence in a moment, was gradually perfected in its various parts. Thus the souls of God's people are regenerated purely by the sovereign will of God and entirely through the agency of his Word and Spirit."[2]

And again,

"The Spirit originally breathed on the face of the waters and reduced the chaotic mass to order and beauty. So does he move upon the believer's soul."[3]

And rather more tentatively,

"Methinks there is some analogy between the first creation of all things, and this new creation which takes place in the soul of man."[4]

The creation of the cosmos and the re-creation of man in Jesus Christ were not, however, isolated acts of the Word and the Spirit. During the interim period of the Fall and the Atonement the work of the Spirit was to prepare the way for our Lord as the promised Messiah.

"It was by the Holy Ghost that Christ spake in the ministry of Noah to the antedeluvian world,[5] and instructed all his people in the wilderness.[6] It was by the Holy Ghost that he moved the prophets in succeeding ages to declare future events,[7] and especially to predict his sufferings, and the glory that should follow."[8]

Simeon thought of the co-operation of the Spirit with the Word as a continuous act of God in history from creation onwards, the whole period of the Old Testament revelation being the essential *praeparatio evangelica* for the final revelation and the Christian Church in which it was to issue. While this is to be understood as an implicit trinitarianism in the Old Testament, we are reminded

---

[1] St John 1.1–14; chs. 14–16 *passim*; 3.1–36.
[2] Sermon 2021—"The Christian A New Creature."
[3] Sermon 2379—"Offices of the Holy Trinity."
[4] Sermon 1117—"Outpouring of the Spirit on the Jews."
[5] 1 Pet. 3.18–20.   [6] Neh. 9.20.   [7] 2 Pet. 1.21.
[8] Sermon 1863—"The Offices of the Holy Spirit."

of the profound theory of Father Lionel Thornton that there is in all spiritual insight an essential element of repetition which, to those who have eyes to see it, reveals the unchanging pattern of divine activity. It is the same God revealing himself yesterday, to-day, and for ever.

Being convinced of the indications of the co-operation of the Spirit with the Word throughout the period of the Old Covenant, Simeon regarded the Lucan and Matthean nativity narratives as providing a further demonstration of it as the pattern for the New Covenant. He accepted the evidence for the conception of the Incarnate Lord "in Holy Spirit", as pointing to the only possible beginning to the New Age which was to be sustained by the Creator-Spirit at every stage. But it was not merely in the conception of the Son of God as Son of Man that his work was to be seen, for it was he who "qualified the man Jesus for his work, and upheld him in it, and wrought miracles by him in confirmation of his mission and raised him up from the dead, and bore witness to him in a visible manner on the day of Pentecost".[1]

At his Baptism, our Lord "was consecrated to his prophetic office by a visible unction of the Holy Spirit";[2] and was driven by the same Spirit to face the temptation of the devil,[3] "and by that same Spirit was enabled to vanquish that mighty foe".[4] Having, therefore, as man defeated the evil one in himself by the power of the Spirit of Holiness, Jesus was able to defeat him in others.

"It was by the Spirit that Christ cast out devils and performed his other miracles."[5] "By the same divine Agent also was he assisted in offering himself a sacrifice upon the cross; for 'through the Eternal Spirit, he offered himself without spot to God'."[6]

By him also was he resurrected, for "the Spirit raised him from the dead and thereby declared him to be the Son of God with power".[7] So finally the Ascension and Pentecost fall naturally into place as the culminating triumphs of a life whose purpose was union with God.

"As conquerors in their triumphs were wont to scatter gifts and largesses among the people, so he received from his heavenly

[1] Sermon 165—"The Law of Purification."
[2] Sermon 1004—"Christ's Commission."   [3] St Mark 1.12.
[4] Sermon 1863—"The Offices of the Holy Spirit."
[5] Sermon 1701—"The Personality and Offices of the Holy Spirit."
[6] Sermon 119—"The Burnt Offering."
[7] Sermon 2230—"The Great Mystery of Godliness."

Father the Holy Spirit, and poured him forth upon the Church in all his gifts and graces."[1]

Although Simeon could not be expected to use modern terminology in describing this co-operation of the Son and the Holy Spirit, what he believed in effect was that this pattern of Christ's Incarnation was the pattern for his Church as the extension of that Incarnation. As the Holy Spirit co-operated with the Lord in his Incarnate life, and as Christ is the pioneer of his redeemed community as well as its Lord, it follows that the Holy Spirit is intended to be the dynamic in us, and Pentecost must follow crucifixion as surely as resurrection. This Simeon emphasized over and over again, in a variety of ways.

"As Christ is ALL in procuring salvation *for* us, so the Holy Spirit is ALL in imparting salvation *to* us."[2]

Indeed, the Incarnation may be fittingly described as "the Holy Spirit co-operating with the Lord Jesus Christ in effecting the redemption of a ruined world",[3] for the revelation of that Incarnation, culminating in Atonement as reconciliation through forgiveness of sins, in resurrection as the guarantee of God's victory, and in Pentecost as the dynamic moment of re-creation, is that there is One God in Three Persons and that he is love. This is the basic statement of the New Testament record of the unique revelation which the Church of the Spirit was to proclaim in the power of the Spirit for evermore; namely, "to make known the offices of the Sacred Three in the economy of redemption; setting forth *the Father* as the Fountain from whence it flows: (for it was from the love he bare to man that he gave us his only dear Son to save us:)[4] and exhibiting *his Son*, his co-equal, co-eternal Son, as our Mediator, through whose obedience unto death our peace with God is obtained: and setting forth *the Holy Ghost* as the Agent, who applies to our souls all the blessings which Christ has purchased for us. This mystery, I say, we are to unfold with all possible clearness and energy: and we must insist upon it as the only foundation of a sinner's hope".[5]

The work of the Holy Spirit, like the work of Christ, is to be seen as the clue to his Person, and although Simeon was ever

[1] Sermon 2108—"The Ascension of Christ."
[2] Sermon 1329—"God's Readiness to Give His Holy Spirit."
[3] Sermon 165—"The Law of Purification."   [4] St John 3.16.
[5] Sermon 1415—"The Apostles' Commission."

concerned to preach "Christ crucified", the Spirit was never far away. Indeed the work of the Holy Spirit, both in the Church and in the individual who is part of it, is necessary before men may come to know Christ as Lord; but although this work of the Spirit is therefore subordinate to the work of Christ, there is no subordination with regard to their Persons. Simeon evidently appreciated what Canon Fison has since called the Spirit's "incurable tendency to self-effacement",[1] which is manifest from the fact that where the Spirit is most certainly present, there we invariably see Christ and not the Spirit, since it is his work to take of the things of Christ and show them to us.

"To this very hour does the Spirit bear the same part 'convincing the world of sin, of righteousness, and of judgement', in order to magnify Christ and to enlarge his kingdom."[2]

We have come, at the end of our enquiry, to Simeon's insistence on the vital place of the Holy Spirit in the life of the Church and of the individual Christian. As the Spirit was in Christ, so is he intended to be in us; and the wholeness of this doctrine of the indwelling Spirit may be summed up in his epigram:

"As Christ died for all, so does the Holy Spirit strive with all."[3]

The Prevenient Spirit is at work wherever men begin to look to Christ for salvation, and the purpose of his striving with men, especially through the medium of the Word of God as proclaimed in the Church, is to bring about their re-creation in Christ, which grows in, and is expressed through, the means of grace during a lifetime of sanctification. This, as he constantly pointed out, is the purpose of the Incarnation, and it leads to the conclusion "that we must seek the renewing influences of the Spirit because our nature is altogether corrupt. . . . When, therefore, we hear of the indispensable necessity of being born again, and of the impossibility of being saved except by faith in Christ, let us remember that these are not the dogmas of a party, but doctrines consequent upon our fallen state, and therefore of universal and infinite importance".[4]

Man, alienated from God by self-will, needs a new nature which can only be created by the Son and the Spirit in accordance with

[1] J. E. Fison, *The Blessing of the Holy Spirit*, 1950, p. 11.
[2] Sermon 1701—"The Personality and Office of the Holy Spirit."
[3] Sermon 2459—"The Believer's Resemblance to God in Love."
[4] Sermon 1861—"Vileness and Impotency of the Natural Man."

the will of the Father; and since he is enabled to return to God through the reconciling ministry of the Son, and enter into a new life through the power of the Spirit of Holiness, it may be said that "the glorification of sinful man is the grand end, for the accomplishing of which the Sacred Three co-operate and concur".[1]

Hence, in this act of God in the individual, the work of the Spirit may be described as being "the efficient cause of our redemption".[2] As man's salvation is not procured by his own efforts, but by the work of Christ in the atonement, so he cannot participate in its benefits by his own power, but by the indwelling of the Holy Spirit who has been revealed for that purpose.

With such a dynamic view of the Person and Work of the Holy Spirit, we should not be surprised to learn that Simeon chose this as the subject for a course of four sermons,[3] which he preached before the University of Cambridge in November 1831, at the age of seventy-two, just five years before his death. Here he set out a clear Biblical statement of the Person of the Spirit, followed by an exhaustive consideration of the Work of the Spirit in the individual. But it must be added that he had not forgotten the work of the Spirit in the Church, for he understood very clearly that the work of the Son and the Spirit in redemption inevitably resulted in the founding of the Church as the community of the redeemed, and that it was a true insight which designated Pentecost the birthday of the Church as the Body of Christ indwelt by by the Spirit of Christ. He regarded the *koinonia* of the Spirit in the many as the ground and expression of actual unity in Christ; God himself at work welding the infinite variety of individuals into a perfect unity. On the vertical plane it is, of course, the communion of the individual "in the Spirit" with the Father through the Son. It must be said that Simeon was more concerned to speak of this latter aspect than of the former because it was the Cinderella of Anglican theology in his day; but both aspects are present, as we may prove for ourselves by the simple expedient of reading his sermons. Ultimately neither is primary, for they are, by their very nature, co-existent and come into being at the same moment; for to be born into sonship of God is to be born into the Church of his Son and of his Spirit.

[1] Sermon 2264—"The Work of the Trinity in Redemption."
[2] Ibid.   [3] Sermons 1863–6.

Two quotations will suffice to summarize Simeon's attitude to the "enthusiasts" on the one hand, whose views on the Holy Spirit led them outside the fellowship of the Church; and to the Bishop Butlers on the other hand, who had so rationalized the doctrine that it was a mere dead letter. Of the "enthusiast " he said:

"I am not, however, without a consciousness, and with deep grief I utter it, that, under a profession of bringing forth only scriptural truth, some give vent to the veriest absurdities, talking about dreams and visions, and arrogating to themselves I know not what claims of preternatural endowments. But against all such fancies and conceits, I would enter my most solemn protest."[1]

At the same time, Simeon refused to admit that such abuses of the scriptural doctrine of the Holy Spirit meant that all references to the subject were to be dismissed; for there existed an even larger group of Christians who, like the twelve men of Ephesus, "did not so much as hear whether the Holy Ghost was given".[2] Of these Simeon said:

"While Christianity *in general* is allowed to be both good and necessary, there is scarcely any regard paid to its *particular*, and most distinguishing tenets. Its fundamental doctrines, such as original sin, justification by faith, regeneration by the Holy Spirit, are discarded as erroneous; and its most essential precepts of holiness and self-denial are ridiculed as preciseness and enthusiasm."[3]

Faced with these two errors, the one going too far, and the other not far enough, it was inevitable that Simeon should emphasize what he considered to be the scriptural statement of the work of the Holy Spirit in the individual; firstly to correct the highly individualistic pneumatic teachers who flouted Church Order; and secondly, to restore to his own communion an article of the Catholic Faith which was being neglected to the detriment of her faith and practice.

III

We have come a long way from the opening question, Where is God my Maker? but enough has been said to show that the answer

[1] Sermon 1866—"The Spirit's Work in Believers."
[2] Acts 19.2.R.V.　　[3] Sermon 1322—"The Single Eye."

given by Simeon, while it was entirely scriptural and orthodox, was never dull and might well be regarded as profoundly stimulating when he came to consider the place of the Third Person of the Blessed and Undivided Trinity. Dr Nuttall has said that the doctrine of the Spirit "received a more thorough and detailed consideration from the Puritans in seventeenth-century England than it has received at any other time in Christian history".[1] But it is equally true that it was central for Simeon, and many like him, at the end of the eighteenth century and at the beginning of the nineteenth in the Church of England. His opening words when he came to preach the first of his series of four sermons on the subject in Great St Mary's were an eloquent attempt to prevent his learned audience from dismissing his apostolic insistence on it as being "little better than an enthusiastic conceit". For not only do they insist upon the priority of religious experience over mere academic theology, but they also place the doctrine in its proper relation to the complete and historical revelation which is the fullness of the catholic doctrine of the Triune God. As we began our inquiry by hearing Simeon speak to us at length on his doctrine of God, we end by allowing him the privilege of repeating his words once more.

"It is an indisputable fact, that we are, by nature, altogether alienated from the life of God. Now we all feel, that, when alienated from a fellow-creature, however we may bear with him in a crowd, we are indisposed to have much personal intercourse with him alone. So, also we feel in reference to God. We can hear of him at a distance and not be disturbed: but, by reason of our alienation from him, we are averse to be brought into very near communion with him. We can bear with a display of his perfections *in the universe*, because, though we see him *as our Creator*, he is not sufficiently near to us to exercise any material controul [*sic*] over us: but when he is brought nigh to us *in the law, as our Governor*, we feel somewhat of a painful constraint, because of our responsibility to him, and the account we must one day give of ourselves to him at his tribunal. Let him then be brought still nearer to us *in the Gospel*, as *our incarnate and suffering God*, and our inquietude is proportionably increased; because we are made to realize more deeply the terrors of his wrath, which demanded such a sacrifice, and the personal obligation which lies upon us to

[1] G. F. Nuttall, *The Holy Spirit in Puritan Faith and Experience*, 1946, p. viii.

surrender up ourselves unreservedly to him. But, in the offices and operations of the Holy Spirit, we are led to view him, not merely as *God, in the universe*, displaying himself *around us*; or as *God, in his Church*, declaring his will *to us*; or as *God, in our nature*, interposing *for us*; but as *God, in our hearts*, dwelling and operating *in us*: and this brings him into such immediate contact with us, and requires of us such a minute attention to all our ways, that we shrink back from every part of the subject, and, for the pacifying of our own minds, cast reflections upon it as visionary, unintelligible, absurd. . . . Men do not like to have God too near to them: and the nearer he is brought to them, the more they show their aversion to that which is the means of presenting him to their minds."[1]

[1] Sermon 1863—"The Offices of the Holy Spirit."

4

SIMEON'S PASTORAL THEOLOGY

DOUGLAS WEBSTER

Simeon's Pastoral Theology

BEFORE ALL else Charles Simeon is remembered and honoured as a preacher and a pastor. For him the priesthood of the Anglican ministry meant two predominant concerns: the Word of God and the souls of men. His immense influence resulted from the quality of his preaching and the power of his personal dealing with men. Few others can have combined in so rare a degree these two gifts of ministry. In our modern theological jargon we should say that he was involved in the problem of communication, though it was less of a problem for him than it is for us, and he was a master of the art. That most of his sermons, so diligently prepared and written out, leave us unmoved and arouse only a few flickers of interest is of no account. He knew the wave-length of his generation. They listened: they responded.

The supreme *motif* of Simeon's ministry can best be described in the words of the Ordinal, which he sought to fulfil point by point. It was "to teach, and to premonish, to feed and provide for the Lord's family; to seek for Christ's sheep that are dispersed abroad, and for his children who are in the midst of this naughty world, that they may be saved through Christ for ever". The Ordinal commits the Anglican priest to being an evangelist, a pastor, and a director of souls. Simeon discharged his responsibility with distinction in all three rôles. All three alike are needed by the faithful if they are to be "saved through Christ for ever". Simeon preached salvation. It was he more than any other who re-introduced this kind of preaching in Anglican pulpits and particularly in the University of Cambridge. At first it was highly unpopular and suspect, but such was the wisdom and perseverance of Simeon that he won the day and changed the prevailing fashion. In a memorial sermon preached by Thomas Webster at St Botolph's, Cambridge, on the Sunday after Simeon's death, it is denied that his later popularity was due to his modifying his views and becoming more guarded in his expressions and assertions. "A vast change has taken place, but the change has

73

been in others, not in him." In his early years doctrines like justification by faith without the works of the law, renewal and sanctification by the influence of the Holy Spirit, were rarely preached and were regarded as Calvinistic, Methodistical, enthusiastic, but now they were very generally maintained and propagated.[1]

Simeon not only preached salvation; by his pastoral care and personal contacts with men he aimed at leading them into the fullness of this experience and seeing that they neither neglected so great a salvation nor fell away from it. This confronts us at once with the celebrated Calvinist-Arminian controversy which raged throughout the eighteenth century and to which the Evangelicals were specially sensitive. Characteristically Simeon refused to identify himself with either party. He pioneered a new and better way. He deplored all systems and would-be systematizers. "He conceived early in life the design of founding a school of *Biblicism*, if the term may be employed."[2] It was because he aimed at teaching "Scriptural Divinity" (we should call it Biblical Theology) that he was able to take a detached and constructive attitude to this controversy, the implications of which could have so great an effect on a man's ministry, particularly on his attitude to preaching and to persons.

Simeon had plenty to say on this issue—in his letters, his sermons, and his conversation parties. It was not a matter of mere academic arguing for him. It went to the root of all that he understood evangelism to be, and it was a burning problem for all his contemporaries, related to almost every aspect of this life and the next. Turning to Scripture as his authority Simeon found that both Calvinism and Arminianism could claim some support but that both failed to take account of certain other passages of Scripture. His general attitude is summed up in one of his notable, if exaggerated, aphorisms: "Both are right in all they affirm and wrong in all they deny." Perhaps Simeon may be pardoned for a trace of vanity in reporting that Dr Coplestone, the Provost of Oriel, "was struck with this remark of mine and assented to it". He generously admits that "there is much more of the right kind

---

[1] A Sermon by Thomas Webster, Rector of St Botolph's, Cambridge, at St Botolph's on 20 November 1836. *The Christian Journal*, 1 February 1837.
[2] Recollections of the Rev. Charles Simeon by the Rt. Rev. Daniel Wilson, D.D., Lord Bishop of Calcutta, in Carus, p. 800.

of orthodoxy at Oxford, as a general rule, than there is here. The Oxford divines frequently err in the nature of regeneration, but are not nearly so far from evangelical truth as is generally the case here".[1] "I think that religious people are too much addicted to human systems. Scarcely anyone is aware that Calvinism and Arminianism are equally true, if rightly applied, and equally false, if pressed to extremes."[2] Simeon regarded himself as "a moderate Calvinist" and as such he thought the great mass of Calvinists to be wrong.[3] He said that he was strongly Calvinistic in some respects and as strongly Arminian in others, being "free from all the trammels of human systems".[4] His duty was not to reconcile each apparently conflicting passage of Scripture but to preach it. "It is by coming to the Scriptures with this mind, that I have been led into the views which I maintain, and which no other person, as far as I am informed, has ever ventured to maintain, in relation to the Calvinistic and Arminian controversy."[5] One of his intentions in publishing his sermons was "to weaken at least, if not to eradicate, the disputes about Calvinism and Arminianism; and thus to recommend, to the utmost of my power, the unhampered liberality of the Church of England".[6] We should recognize, however, that Simeon's teaching is by no means a watered-down version of the two opposing systems. He would almost certainly have agreed with some recent words of Dr A. R. Vidler: "A theology of reconciliation or of comprehension does not mean a theology of moderation, of the *juste milieu*, of sitting on the fence, of nerveless indecision. That is what it may rot away into. But, rightly understood and in its genuine representatives, it is a theology not of fog or haze, but of thunder and lightning; a theology which comes down off the fence, but not always on the same side, and which certainly does not fall into a copy-book place on a party line."[7] That was true of Simeon.[8]

[1] Brown, p. 267.

[2] Letter to a Clergyman, 2 July 1833, quoted in Carus, p. 725.

[3] Letter to the Rev. W. Carus Wilson, 11 October 1815, quoted in Carus, pp. 418f.   [4] Op. cit., p. 563.

[5] Letter to Bishop Burgess, 24 October 1820, quoted in Carus, p. 540.

[6] Op. cit., p. 719.

[7] A. R. Vidler, *Essays in Liberality*, 1957, pp. 168f. Cf. E. M. Forster: "Truth, being alive, was not half-way between anything. It was only to be found by continuous excursions into either realm, and though proportion is the final secret, to espouse it at the outset is to ensure sterility." *Howard's End* (Penguin edition), p. 182.

[8] Others of the more moderate evangelical churchmen were equally

6

Simeon's main criticisms were directed against Calvinism. This was partly because he regarded it as a far graver menace among the Anglican Evangelicals of his day, the great majority of these being Calvinists, and partly because its extreme positions simply could not be held in the light of his own pastoral experience. He, like Cecil and Pratt and many of the founders of the Church Missionary Society, was immersed in practical theology; they could not hold academic views which would not fit the realities of the human situation. In pastoral terms the main elements of this theological debate can be distilled into certain basic doctrines:

1. Predestination and Election.
2. The Perseverance (or indefectibility) of the Saints.
3. Assurance.

Let us consider Simeon's views on each of these in turn.

1. Simeon is reported to have said in conversation:

"I call myself neither a predestinarian nor an anti-predestinarian, but I commit myself to the inspired writing, whatever complexion it may assume. . . . When I come to a text which speaks of election, I delight myself in the doctrine of election. When the Apostles exhort me to repentance and obedience, and indicate my freedom of choice and action, I give myself up to that side of the question. Don't you know, my dear brother, that the wheels of your watch move in opposite directions? Yet they are all tending to one result."[1]

It seems that when he was a very young man he found the doctrine of election a difficulty and at first could not receive it, "not being able to separate it from that of reprobation. . . . But I soon critical of "systematizing", as they called it. There was a discussion on this subject at a meeting of the Eclectic Society on 14 May 1810 when Josiah Pratt urged that "Scripture will not bend to refined systems. For example, pardon and justification are not so clearly distinguished in Scripture as in human systems". Richard Cecil repeatedly makes the same point. "The right way of interpreting Scripture is to take it as we find it, without any attempt to force it into any particular system. Many passages speak the language of what is called Calvinism, and that in almost the strongest terms: I would not have a man clip and curtail these passages, to bring them down to some system: let him go with them in their full and free sense; for otherwise, if he do not absolutely pervert them, he will attenuate their energy. But let him look at as many more, which speak the language of Arminianism, and let him go all the way with these also. God has been pleased thus to state and to leave the thing; and all attempts to distort it, one way or the other, are puny and contemptible." (Richard Cecil's *Remains*, pp. 458f.)

[1] Memorandum by J. J. Gurney, April 1831, quoted in Carus, pp. 673ff.

learned that I must take the Scriptures with the simplicity of a little child, and be content to receive on God's testimony what he has revealed, whether I can unravel all the difficulties that may attend it or not".[1] From that time he never doubted the doctrine of election, though he did not state it in extreme forms nor press it to the logical conclusions of the advanced Calvinists. In one of his sermons he says:

"It is undeniable that the apostles mention occasionally, and without the smallest appearance of hesitation, the doctrines of predestination and election. . . . We are aware that great difficulties attend the explanation of these doctrines; (though certainly no greater than attend the denial of them:) and we are aware also that they are open to abuse"—but so is every other doctrine. He goes on to suggest that by predestination "we are not to imagine that (God) is actuated by arbitrary volition", and that predestination is not hostile to the interests of morality because its end is "that we should be holy". "God has not chosen us because *we were* holy, or because he foresaw *we should become* holy, but *in order that we might be* holy: he has chosen us to holiness as *the means*, as well as to glory as *the end*. . . . Wherever election and predestination are spoken of, they are spoken of in this view, as having respect to holiness, and as assuring to us the attainment of holiness. . . . When once we see that (these deep mysterious truths) secure infallibly the attainment of holiness in the way to glory, and that no man is entitled to think himself one of God's elect, any farther than the holiness of his life bears testimony to him, we shall soon renounce our prejudices, and willingly concede to sovereign grace the whole glory of our salvation."

Simeon defended these doctrines on the ground that they made salvation wholly the work of God. Did not Archbishop William Temple make much the same point in his celebrated discussion on Grace and Freedom when he wrote: "All is of God; the only thing of my very own which I can contribute to my own redemption is the sin from which I need to be redeemed"?[2] But Simeon sympathizes with those who cannot go all the way with him and in the same sermon adds: "We are far from thinking that the doctrines of election and predestination are of primary and fundamental importance. We well know that many eminently pious

---

[1] Carus, p. 25.
[2] W. Temple, *Nature, Man and God*, 1934, p. 401.

persons have not been able to receive them: and we have no doubt but that a person may serve God most acceptably though he should not have an insight into these mysterious truths." Those who can accept them are to enjoy them but not unnecessarily to obtrude them upon others.[1]

Simeon goes out of his way to deny that the doctrine of election implies that of reprobation. All our knowledge of these mysteries derives from revelation, and that revelation does not allow the doctrine of absolute reprobation "I think it as clear as the light itself. If when Almighty God swears by his own life and immortal perfections, that 'he has not pleasure in the death of a sinner, but rather that he should turn from his wickedness and live' . . . I am constrained to say, that the doctrine of absolute reprobation, that is, of God's forming any persons with an express determination to destroy them, irrespectively of any works of theirs, cannot be true."[2] Simeon approaches this subject as a pastor concerned with sick souls. The doctrine of election should encourage people, it is "the best possible antidote to despair".

Elsewhere he remarks that this is a subject not to be entered upon without extreme caution. "To be bringing it forward on every occasion, just as if it were among the first principles of religion, we consider as very injudicious, and detrimental to the best interests of religion: but to omit it altogether we deem unworthy of a faithful servant of Christ." On the other hand, "If any man be not able to receive this doctrine, we would on no account press it upon his mind: we would rather say to him, Discard it from your mind, and take the broad promises of Scripture, wherein it is declared, that 'the blood of Jesus Christ cleanseth from all sin' and that he 'will save to the uttermost all who come unto God by him'. Take, I say, these promises, not with any reference whatever to God's eternal counsels toward you personally, but with a perfect confidence that he will fulfil them to all who rely upon him; and that no sinner in the universe, who comes to him in his Son's name, shall ever be cast out."[3] Again we see the love of the pastor prevailing over the logic of academic theology. Simeon would have agreed with a later and far greater

[1] All above quotations from Sermon 2092—"Thanks to God for His Sovereign Grace and Mercy."
[2] Sermon 2379—"The Offices of the Holy Trinity."
[3] Sermon 1878—"Predestination Considered."

theologian, P. T. Forsyth, who once admitted: "I could not contemplate academic conclusions without asking how they would affect these people and my word to them in doubt, death, grief, or repentance. . . . They were in no spiritual condition to have forced on them those questions on which scholars so delighted and differed."[1]

Simeon's most positive line of approach to this problem is along the lines of God's love. We are "drawn" to God. "The drawings of God's Spirit do not in the least interfere with the liberty of human actions. . . . It is 'with the cords of a man and with the bands of love'; it is through the medium of the understanding, the will and the affections; the understanding as enlightened with divine truth; the will as determined by sound judgement; and the affections as engaged by the excellence of those things which the will is bent to follow. True, it is, that we cannot precisely declare the manner in which the operations of the Holy Spirit influence the soul; for we do not even know how our own spirit acts upon the body: but we know infallibly, that God does influence the minds of men; not however by making them to act contrary to their will, but by making them 'willing in the day of his power' (Psalm 110.3)." Again he pleads that people should not look on the dark side of this question and think what will become of them if they are not elect. Instead of contemplating God's sovereignty in connection only with justice, they should contemplate the sovereignty of his love and mercy. "If they turned their thoughts more to his *everlasting love*, they would soon feel its attractive and constraining influence. . . . You will then soon find a sweet confidence springing up in your souls; you will look to him as a Father; you will regard him as a Friend; you will feel encouragement to cast yourselves upon him, and pleasure in giving up yourselves in his service."[2] It takes little imagination to realize how great must have been the influence of a man who could preach with such warmth and humanity as this.

2. On the much-debated question about the possibility of a true Christian falling into apostasy Simeon comes down strongly on the Arminian side. He taught that the Calvinist doctrine "once a Christian always a Christian" (in more technical language "the

---

[1] P. T. Forsyth, *Positive Preaching and the Modern Mind*, 1907, p. 282.
[2] Sermon 1068—"Gracious Influences the Fruit of Election."

final perseverance of the saints") could not be maintained in that form, because Scripture had so many warnings about apostasy. Simeon makes it clear that he did not enjoy criticizing the Calvinist position, and he submits that though it had been severely assaulted times without number by enemies, here it is "wounded by a friend", adding "I believe in final perseverance as much as any of them; but not in *the way* that others do. God's purpose shall stand; but our liability to fall and perish is precisely the same as ever it was: our security, as far as it relates to Him, consists in *faith*; and, as far as it relates to ourselves, it consists in *fear*".[1]

Simeon makes the interesting observation "that whilst Calvinists complain of Arminians as unfair and unscriptural, in denying *personal*, though they admit *national*, election, they themselves are equally unfair and unscriptural in denying the danger of *personal* apostasy, whilst they admit it in reference to churches and nations. It is lamentable to see the plain statements of Scripture so unwarrantably set aside for the maintaining of human systems".[2]

On this matter we see again how Simeon's approach is pastoral. "It would not indeed be expedient for *young converts* to indulge too strong a confidence; because their sincerity has been but little tried, and they are by no means sufficiently simple in their dependence on God: in proportion therefore as the evidences of their faith are defective and the means of stability are overlooked, they must relax their confidence of persevering to the end. As for those who are already in a backslidden state, it would be a most horrible delusion in them to say, that nothing should separate them from the love of God; since they have reason to doubt at this moment whether they be at all interested in his love." The only person who can have such confidence is "a humble contrite person, that is living by faith in the Son of God, and maintaining a suitable conversation in all his spirit and conduct".[3]

In another sermon Simeon goes further than this. He is preaching on the text: "Now the just shall live by faith: but if any man draw back, my soul shall have no pleasure in him. But we are not of them who draw back to perdition; but of them that believe to the saving of the soul."[4] Simeon begins: "On few passages of Scripture do we behold more glaring perversions than in comments upon these words. Some, in order to uphold a favourite

[1] Carus, pp. 566f.   [2] Carus, p. 566n.
[3] Sermon 1882—"Paul's Assurance of Perseverance."   [4] Hebrews 10.38,39.

system, will deny that the persons here cautioned against apostasy are the same as are spoken of in the preceding and following context. But I entreat you, brethren, never to wrest the Word of God. Take the Word as little children without enquiring what human system it appears to favour; and let it have all the force which it evidently bears in the passage from whence it is taken: and if you cannot reconcile different parts of God's blessed Word, leave that to him, saying, 'What I know not now, I shall know hereafter'. It is plain that every man, whatever his attainments be, has need of this solemn warning: it is evident beyond all contradiction that many, after having long professed to believe in Christ, have gone back and made shipwreck of their faith: and Paul himself felt a need of exercising continual watchfulness and self-denial, 'lest after having preached to others he himself should be a castaway'." At the same time Simeon, with a priest's concern for the souls of his people, goes on to say: "Though the danger of falling is such as may excite in us a holy watchfulness, it need not generate in us a slavish fear: since God engages to uphold the upright in heart, and they are therefore warranted in expecting from Him all needful aid."[1]

Simeon preached on the dangers of apostasy and criticized the Calvinist position again and again. "It is affirmed by some that there is in true believers an indefectible principle of grace which renders it impossible for them to fall. . . . I do not conceive that there is or ever was upon the face of the whole earth a man who could say, 'I have within me an indefectible principle of grace, so that I cannot fall or cannot perish'." What irked Simeon was the "cannot"; he would have preferred "will not". And he does not base his hope of perseverance on the necessary or irresistible influence of grace already received. "I admit that he (the converted Christian) *shall* be kept from falling. . . . I assert that he is *in himself* as liable to fall as ever, and that it is from an *extrinsic source* he derives all his stability: and that consequently, whilst he has the strongest possible hope in God, he ought to keep in abiding and undiminished exercise and holy fear: yea more, I must say, that if once he lose that fear and become self-confident, he is already on the very verge of destruction." Simeon produces a rather telling illustration of Christian stability, that of a kite "soaring on high in a situation foreign to its nature as the soul

[1] Sermon 2316—"The True Means of Perseverance."

of man is when raised above this lower world to high and heavenly pursuits". At a distance one cannot see how the kite is kept in position, seeing neither the wind nor the string nor the hand that holds. The kite has nothing in itself to uphold itself; if left for one moment to itself it would fall, because it has the same tendency to gravitate to earth that it always had. So with the soul of the believer. It is raised by the Spirit of God to a preternatural state and upheld by his invisible almighty hand through the medium of faith. "And upheld it shall be; but not by any power inherent in itself." At one point, as Simeon himself admits, the illustration breaks down. The kite is upheld without any concurrence of its own, whereas the soul, notwithstanding its entire dependence on God, does yet in fact "work out its own salvation", and therefore the believer's concurrence is necessary. The Calvinist would encourage confidence alone; Simeon would encourage humility and holy fear. He has the same faith that the Calvinist has, believing the promise of our Lord that none should pluck his sheep out of his hand, but instead of allowing this to engender presumption, false confidence, and moral indifferentism, Simeon insists that it must produce the reverse.[1]

One cause of apostasy, in Simeon's view, is the neglecting to advance in religion. Expounding Hebrews 6.4–6 he shows how even the enlightened and those who have considerable spiritual powers can become apostates from the truth. Commenting on the words "it is impossible . . . to renew them again unto repentance" he says that we are to understand this not as an absolute impossibility but only as a moral impossibility, and he explains what might seem to be theological hairsplitting by citing our Lord's words that all things are possible with God, even though impossible with men (St Matthew 19.26). "Thus the recovery of such apostates is quite contrary to all reasonable expectation; nor can anything but a most extraordinary interposition of the Deity effect it."[2] Simeon pointed out that a man does not suddenly become an apostate. First he indulges some secret sin, then he declines into formality in his walk with God, then the besetting sin gets ascendancy, then he becomes indifferent to public ordinances, and so from opposing the Gospel in his heart

[1] Sermon 2439—"True Grounds of a Christian's Stability."
[2] Sermon 2290—"The Danger of Apostasy." Simeon repeats this distinction in Sermon 2425 in a cross reference to this passage.

and life he comes to abandon it even in profession, to relapse into avowed infidelity and contempt of all true religion.[1] In one of his conversation parties at which this subject was under discussion Simeon suggested that Luther, Melanchthon, and others, in emerging from popery went too far in the opposite extreme. Simeon was less concerned with the tying up of loose theological ends in this problem than with giving Scriptural direction to the souls in his charge, warning them of the dangers both of presumption and backsliding.

3. On the doctrine of assurance he stands at a considerable distance from the Wesleys. This seems to have troubled him more in his earlier than his later life. As a young man he had read the writings of James Hervey, one of the members of the Holy Club at Oxford to which the Wesleys had belonged, and had been much perplexed by Hervey's views on the nature of saving faith. On the advice of one of his father's friends, Dr Loveday of Caversham, he borrowed a volume of Archbishop Sharp's sermons. "These I read with great profit; they shewed me that Hervey's view of saving faith was erroneous: and from that day to this I have never had a doubt upon the subject. I think it is clear, even to demonstration, that *assurance* is not necessary to saving faith; a simple reliance on Christ for salvation is that faith which the word of God requires; assurance is a privilege but not a duty." Simeon proceeds to make a distinction between assurance of faith and assurance of hope (cf. Hebrews 10.22 and 6.11), stating that a man may possess the first but not the second, for "he may be fully assured of Christ's power and willingness to save him, and yet not be assured that Christ has actually imparted salvation to him. The truth is, that these two kinds of assurance, namely of faith and hope, have respect to very different things; assurance of faith having a respect only to the truth of God in his word, whilst assurance of hope is founded on the correspondence of our character with that of the word: the one believes that God will fulfil his promises to persons of a particular description; and the other, that we ourselves are of that very character to whom they are and shall be fulfilled".[2]

In a paper compiled in 1819 Simeon again confesses that he was

[1] Sermon 2313—"The Evil and Danger of Apostasy."
[2] Carus, pp. 14–16, from a personal memoir written by Simeon in 1813.

misled by Mr Hervey on saving faith and that he had now found
it was a faith of affiance and not of assurance. Since realizing this
he had had peace, "because though I had not faith of assurance,
I had as full a conviction that I relied on the Lord Jesus Christ
alone for salvation, as I had of my own existence"—and from that
time on he had never lost this hope and confidence in the Saviour.
Since sin and salvation are both alike the experience of the believer, his attitude must combine both humility and thankfulness.
"This is the religion that pervades the whole Liturgy and particularly the Communion service. . . . The repeated cries to each
Person of the ever-adorable Trinity for mercy, are not at all too
frequent or too fervent for me; nor is the confession in the Communion service too strong for me;[1] nor the Te Deum nor the
ascriptions of glory after the Lord's Supper too exalted for me.
. . . This makes the Liturgy as superior to all modern compositions
as the work of a philosopher on any deep subject is to that of a
school-boy who understands scarcely anything about it." Simeon
considered the religion of his day to be defective at the point of
reverence and awe for God, and he suggests that part of the reason
for this was an over-assurance. "The confidence that is generally
professed does not sufficiently, in my opinion, savour of a
creature-like spirit, or of a sinner-like spirit."[2]

Throughout all his long years of preaching and teaching
Simeon never lost his sense of wonder at God's gift of salvation.
He never seems to have doubted the reality of salvation for himself, but he spoke of his own salvation "as of that which would
be the very masterpiece of Divine grace, and of the probability
of his being the last and the least in the kingdom of heaven".[3]
This was why Simeon, though being assured, could never proclaim a glib or easy doctrine of assurance. With Bonhoeffer he
knew that there was no cheap grace. He had meditated on the
great cost of the world's salvation.

*   *   *

[1] It was for John Wesley. See John Bowmer, *The Sacrament of the Lord's
Supper in Early Methodism*, 1951, pp. 209, 212, where it is pointed out that the
words "the remembrance of them [i.e. sins] is intolerable" in the Communion Confession would not fit lips accustomed to sing, "My chains fell
off, my heart was free."

[2] Carus, pp. 518–25.

[3] A memorandum by J. J. Gurney, Carus, p. 681.

Simeon had no clearly worked out soteriology, but his most extensive treatment of the Atonement is to be found in his fourteen sermons on the Fourth Servant Song (Isaiah 52.13—53.12). It would be tedious to quote at any length from these. Let it be sufficient to select certain points in order as the preacher expounded the passage.

1. The work of Christ as God's Servant was:

> To reveal the Father's Will to mankind,
> To make atonement for their sins, and
> To reduce them to a state of holy obedience.[1]

In other words he executed the office of prophet, priest, and king. "He 'fulfilled all righteousness' even though by so doing he made himself appear to be a sinner like unto us. . . . Nor was there any kind of suffering which he did not endure, that he might fully expiate our guilt by bearing in our stead all that our sin had merited."[2]

2. The Cross is the central theme of all Scripture. "This is that mystery in which are contained all the treasures of wisdom and knowledge. It is so extensive a field for meditation, that, though we traverse it ever so often, we need never resume the same track: and it is such a marvellous fountain of blessedness to the soul, that, if we have ever drunk of its refreshing streams, we shall find none other so pleasant to our taste."[3] Christ submitted to the depths of humiliation that he might purge us from the guilt of sin by his blood. "Behold then, ye who are bowed down by a sense of guilt; draw nigh to Calvary, and see the provision made for your salvation."[4]

3. The means of conversion is the preaching of the Gospel. "This was the weapon the apostles used in their warfare. They preached Christ in every place. Jesus and the resurrection was their constant theme. . . . The same must be the constant tenour of our ministrations. There is no other subject that we can insist upon with equal effect. Philosophy leaves men as it finds them: it may afford some glimmering light to their minds; but it can never influence their hearts. Nothing can pull down the strongholds of sin but that which points out a refuge for sinners."[5]

[1] Sermon 963—"Christ Rewarded for His Services."   [2] Ibid.
[3] Sermon 964—"The Depth of our Saviour's Humiliation."   [4] Ibid.
[5] Sermon 965—"The Means and Evidence of Conversion."

4. The fruit or evidence of conversion is that our mouths are shut before the Lord Jesus. We cease vindicating ourselves. Our objections to justification by faith alone are silenced.

5. Expounding the text "Who hath believed our report?" Simeon deals with man's neglect of the Gospel. "All imagine themselves to be believers, and because they have been baptized into the name of Christ, they conceive themselves to be possessed of real faith. But I must say with the Apostle 'Examine yourselves whether ye be in the faith; prove your own selves'. To ascertain the point, I beg you to ask yourselves two questions, namely, *How you obtained your faith?* and *How it operates?* Do not suppose that the faith of Christ is bare assent to truths which you have been taught by your parents, or that it is that kind of conviction that is founded upon a consideration of evidence, such as you would feel respecting any common report which was substantiated to your satisfaction. True 'faith is the gift of God'. . . . Ask yourselves further, How your faith operates? Where it is real, 'it works by love' (Galatians 5.6), and 'overcomes the world' (1 John 5.4) and 'purifies the heart' (Acts 15.9). See then, brethren, whether your faith produces these effects; for if it do not, it is but a 'dead faith', 'the faith of devils'. If you examine yourselves in this way, you will find that there is still the same occasion as ever for the complaint in my text."[1] This quotation might serve to illustrate how Simeon dealt with nominal Christians.

6. The treatment of the Messiah "proves indisputably how men would treat God, if they had him in their power. God has, for the accomplishment of His gracious purposes, condescended to clothe himself in human flesh and to sojourn among men. He assumed nothing of the pomp and splendour of this world, that the attachment or aversion of men might the more evidently appear to arise from their discovery of his true character. He dazzled not their eyes by a full display of his deity, but suffered the rays of it occasionally to appear, as their organs of vision were able to bear it. He admitted them so close to him, that they might easily contemplate his proper character and form a rational judgement of his excellencies and perfections. By this he gave them an opportunity of testifying what were the dispositions of their minds towards him. And what was the result of the experiment? Did they love him, admire him, adore him as God? Behold, they

[1] Sermon 966—"Men's Neglect of the Gospel."

could 'see no form nor comeliness in him'. On the contrary they hated him, despised him, and crucified him as a malefactor".[1]

7. Jesus suffered for the expiating of our guilt
for the effecting of our peace
for the renovating of our nature.[2]

8. "The lost state of man by nature and his recovery through the blood of Christ are the two principal doctrines of our religion." Simeon again describes religious formality and the nominal Christian. "To set an example to those around him, and to be proposed as a pattern to the rising generation, is a far higher satisfaction to him than to riot in dissipation or to amass riches. With these views he is attentive to all the external duties of religion: his prayers, such as they are, are regularly performed in the church, the family, and the closet. A portion of the Scriptures is read at stated seasons: his servants are instructed: his children are catechized: his hand is stretched out to relieve the poor and needy. In short, nothing is omitted that may elevate him in the eyes of others and serve as a foundation for self-complacency. *This* he supposes to be God's way, when in fact it is as much as either the worldling's or the sensualist's, a way of his own: for in all there is nothing of brokenness[3] of heart and contrition, nothing of faith in the Lord Jesus Christ, and nothing of devotedness to the glory of God."[4]

Only the death of Jesus is the means of our restoration. Simeon propounds the traditional theory of penal substitution but, as almost invariably, he confines himself to the words of Scripture and resorts to no crude illustrations or simplifications. "As all the iniquities of all the children of Israel were transferred to the scape-goat under the law, that he might bear them away into a land of oblivion, so were all the sins of the whole human race transferred to Christ, that, having borne the curse due to them, he might take them all away from us for ever." Again, "By the death of Jesus in our stead, our guilt is cancelled, and justice itself is satisfied on our behalf. Moreover, the gift of the Holy Spirit is procured for us, that by his operations, our nature may be changed,

[1] Sermon 967—"The Characters and Treatment of the Messiah."
[2] Sermon 968—"The True Cause of our Lord's Sufferings."
[3] See later, pp. 97ff., for further references to Simeon's teaching on "brokenness".
[4] Sermon 969—"The Means of Man's Restoration to God."

and we may be brought to delight as much in the ways of God as ever we delighted in the ways of sin."[1] It is to be noted that unlike some exponents of the penal view Simeon relates the doctrine of the Atonement closely to that of the Holy Spirit. This would have pleased R. C. Moberly, whose criticism of the traditional view was that it needed the doctrine of the Holy Spirit. "Calvary without Pentecost, would not be an atonement *to us*. But Pentecost could not be without Calvary. Calvary is the possibility of Pentecost: and Pentecost is the realization, in human spirits, of Calvary."[2]

9. Before expounding the central mystery of the Cross, which Simeon not very happily calls "The Father's Conduct Towards Jesus", he wisely warns his hearers against expecting to understand it all. "God never intended that we should; nor indeed is it possible. We know that an ignorant peasant is not able to search out the reasons upon which a profound statesman acts; nor could he comprehend them if they were laid before him: and shall we wonder if there be some mysteries in the revelation and in the providence of God which we cannot explore, and which perhaps, if unfolded ever so clearly, would be far above our comprehension?" Commenting on the words "It pleased the Lord to bruise him" he says: "As the Father did not take pleasure in inflicting punishment, so neither did the Son in enduring it, *for itself*; the punishment, considered separately from its consequences, was equally grievous to him who inflicted and to him who bore it. But Jesus thirsted for the salvation of men." Again, "We are not to suppose that the Son loved us more than the Father; for the Father expressed as much love in giving his Son, as the Son did in giving himself. . . . The whole work of salvation is the fruit of the Father's love."[3] At least Simeon avoids the more extreme crudities of the penal view; he does his best to meet the obvious moral difficulties that it arouses; and he relates the Cross to the doctrine of the Trinity. If the words of the Bible are in any degree to influence one's understanding of the Atonement, it is not possible to dismiss the penal view altogether simply because we do not like the manner in which it has more often than not been stated.

10. We shall hardly be surprised to find that Simeon held a quantitative view of Christ's sufferings, a view which has been

---

[1] Ibid. [2] R. C. Moberly, *Atonement and Personality*, 1924, p. 152.
[3] Sermon 972.

so cogently criticized by P. T. Forsyth. "Christ being God as well as man, there was an infinite value in his sufferings; his sufferings for a time were equivalent to the sufferings of the whole world to all eternity." But despite this Simeon does go on to recognize the atoning value of our Lord's obedience, his holy obedience as Forsyth would have called it. "There was also an infinite value in his obedience; so that it could merit, not for himself only, but for others, yea for all the myriads of sinners who should trust in it." [1]

One of Simeon's most famous sermons is entitled "Evangelical Religion Described". [2] It was preached before the university on 17 March 1811 and was distributed to every parishioner after his death. He begins by the statement that God usually speaks through the ministers of his Word, and that in the text "I determined not to know any thing among you, save Jesus Christ, and him crucified" St Paul declares the scope of his own ministry and the one subject which he laboured to unfold. This was not merely the fact of the crucifixion but the doctrine of it. First, it is the ground of our hope because it is the means of our reconciliation with God and has won us every blessing we possess. Second, it is the motive to our obedience, and in this respect St Paul was no less earnest in promoting the interests of holiness. Taking both together results in affiance in Christ for salvation and a consequent obedience to the law of God for his sake. "If he had neglected to inculcate holiness, and to set forth redeeming love as the great incentive to obedience, he would have been justly chargeable with that which has been often falsely imputed to him—an antinomian spirit." But he kept both.

The sermon then opens out to give the reasons for the apostle's determination. The first was that this subject "contained all that he was commissioned to declare", the ministry of reconciliation. We have the same ministry. On this basis Simeon defends "evangelical" religion. "As though men needed not to be evangelized now, the term *evangelical* is used as a term of reproach. We mean not to justify any persons whatsoever, in using unnecessary terms of distinction, more especially if it be with a view to depreciate others, and to aggrandize themselves: but still the distinctions which are made in Scripture must be made by us; else

[1] Sermon 973—"Christ's Death A Condition of Salvation."
[2] Sermon 1933.

for what end has God Himself made them? ... Here then [the apostle] lays down the distinction between doctrines which are truly evangelical, and others which have no just title to that name." This text is what really constitutes evangelical preaching. The subject of it must be "Christ crucified". Christ must be set forth as the sinner's hope, and holiness "in all its branches" must be enforced. "Thus to preach, and thus to live, would characterize a person and his ministry as evangelical in the eyes of the Apostle: whereas indifference to this doctrine, or a corruption of it, either by a self-righteous or antinomian mixture, would render both the person and his ministry obnoxious to his censure." Simeon goes out of his way to emphasize that he is not wanting to confine the use of the term "evangelical" to any party or system or to deny the usefulness of others in the Church, "but this we say, that in proportion as any persons, in their spirit and in their preaching, accord with the example in the text, they are properly denominated *evangelical*; and that in proportion as they recede from this pattern, their claim to this title is dubious or void. Now then we ask, What is there in this which every minister ought not to preach, and every Christian to feel? Is there anything in this enthusiastic? anything sectarian? anything uncharitable? anything worthy of reproach?"

The second reason for the Apostle's determination was that the preaching of Christ crucified "contained all that could conduce to the happiness of man", whatever his need, whatever his situation. "Let a sense of redeeming love occupy the soul, and the heart becomes enlarged, and 'the feet are set at liberty to run the way of God's commandments'. We say not that every person who *professes* to have experienced the love of Christ will always walk consistently with that profession; for there were falls and offences not only in the apostolic age, but even among the apostles themselves. But this we say, that there is no other principle in the universe so powerful as the love of Christ; that whilst that principle is in action, no commandment will ever be considered as grievous. ... This the Apostle found in his own experience; and this he found to be the effect of his ministry on the heart of thousands."

A further illustration of Simeon's evangelistic preaching may be found in his sermon on The Mediation of Christ.[1] He describes

[1] Sermon 2229.

the text ("a ransom for all")[1] as "a stronghold for those who
adopt the sentiments which are called Arminian" and points out
that the Calvinist gets over them by saying "that by 'all' is meant
some of every description, that is some of all different ranks and
orders of men, Jews and Gentiles, rich and poor. But how much
better were it for men to confess their own ignorance than to
pervert the Word of God. . . . Christ died 'for all' without exception. To say that He died for the elect only is neither Scriptural
nor true. . . . If all be not ultimately saved by his death, it is not
owing to any want of sufficiency in his sacrifice to procure
acceptance for them, but to their own impenitence and unbelief".
Then he makes his appeal. "On your acceptance of this testimony
your everlasting salvation depends. . . . Believe then, every one of
you, that Christ died for *you*; and pray to God, that you may be
able to see your interest in Him, and with joyful confidence to
exclaim 'He hath loved *me* and given himself for ME'. Then shall
you be feasted with the foretaste of heaven, and grow up into an
increasing meetness for the glory prepared for you."

From all this we may infer that Simeon's evangelistic preaching
was founded on two dogmas: first, the need, the sin, and the guilt
of man; second, the love of God as revealed in the saving work
of Christ on Calvary. This was the doctrine of salvation with
which he constantly confronted his congregation. He proclaimed
facts, not theories. Simeon, unlike the Calvinists, believed that
God's salvation was for all. Though not a universalist he loved
the universalist texts and summarized his understanding of
Scripture on this point:

1. For all, without exception, has God given his only Son.
2. To all has he commanded also his Gospel to be preached.
3. Nor is there a human being whom God is not willing to
   receive.[2]

It goes without saying that Simeon preached justification by
faith, by faith alone, but he qualifies this against misunderstanding
and misrepresentation. In a letter to Bishop Dampier of Ely he is
anxious lest the bishop should get wrong information about his
views. "If, for instance, anyone should say that I maintain the
doctrine of Justification by Faith alone, and yet leave an impression on the mind that I neglected to enforce good works; what he

[1] 1 Timothy 2.5,6.   [2] Sermon 2228—"Salvation for All."

might say in words would be substantially true, but in fact it would be as false as if he should accuse me of Socinianism or Deism."[1] Simeon's teaching on justification by faith can be seen in his celebrated university sermon entitled "The Gospel Message".[2] He defines salvation as "the everlasting happiness of the soul" and stresses that it is more than a temporary deliverance. It is to be obtained by faith. "The faith intended is far more than an acknowledgment of the truth of the Gospel; it is an approbation of it as excellent and an acceptance of it as suitable. Assent is an act of the understanding only: but true faith is a consent of the will also, with the full concurrence of our warmest affections," i.e. believing with the heart. The principle of reliance on Christ "takes us off from all self-dependence" but "leads us to purify our hearts from the love and practice of all sin". The man who truly "embraces Christ as a suitable and all-sufficient Saviour" relies on the divine promises, lives in communion with the Saviour, and exerts himself to live a holy life. It is not unreasonable, asserts Simeon, that a person coming to Christ in this penitent manner should be saved. Simeon goes on to imply that this kind of salvation involves a daily renewal, for each is to ask the question, "Do I daily with humility and earnestness beg of God that Christ may be made unto me wisdom and righteousness and sanctification and redemption?" This plan of salvation refers all the glory to Jesus Christ, whereas every other leaves room for man to boast. And it, most of all, secures the practice of good works. Simeon concludes with this appeal to clergy and ordinands. "Be not offended if I ask, whether you yourselves have received the truth in love of it? If you have not, how can you commend it to others? How can it be expected that you should 'contend earnestly for that faith' which you yourselves have never embraced; or that you should labour with becoming zeal to convert your hearers, when you yourselves are unconverted?"

For all his defence of *sola fide* Simeon could also preach on the importance of works—and did. "Faith, of whatever kind it be, is of no value any farther than it is attested by works. If faith in the first instance apprehends Christ as a Saviour from guilt and condemnation, it does not rest there: it lays hold on him for sancti-

---

[1] Carus, p. 275.
[2] This was preached on 13 November 1796 on the text Mark 16.15,16. Five editions of it were published before the end of the year. It is sermon 1461.

fication, as well as for righteousness." St Paul and St James were writing on two different subjects. "St Paul is proving that a man is not to seek salvation by any righteousness of his own but simply by faith in the Lord Jesus Christ: whereas St James is proving that the man who professes to have faith in Christ must shew forth his faith by his works. St Paul is endeavouring to convince the self-justificiary; St James, the antinomian—St Paul by shewing that works are nothing without faith; St James by shewing that faith is nothing without works. St Paul exalts Christ as giving a title to heaven; St James as giving a meetness for heaven. . . . Thus, according to the two Apostles, a man is justified by *faith*, because *by it* he *is made* righteous; and he is justified *by works*, because *by them* he is proved righteous."[1] In another place Simeon goes further still. "We must look to our ways and run with holy diligence the race that is set before us. God's final decision will be the result of our conduct [*sic*!] and not of his decrees. He will never save anyone purely because he had decreed to save him; nor condemn him because he had decreed to make him 'a vessel of wrath'. If he award eternal life to anyone, it will be because he had sought it in Christ, and 'by patient continuance in well doing'; and if anyone be made a monument of God's indignation and wrath, it will be altogether on the ground of his evil deeds, and of his having rejected that Gospel whereby alone he could be saved."[2]

Simeon's views on justification meant fighting a battle on two fronts: against those who pressed "*sola fide*" to a point that amounted to antinomianism, and against those who really believed in salvation by works. Simeon faces this problem in a sermon on "The True Test of Religion in the Soul".[3] He distinguishes explicitly between nominal and real Christians. "It is not by their profession of any principles that we are to judge men's state, but by the practical effect of those principles on their hearts and lives." To this extent Simeon was a spiritual pragmatist. He followed the criterion laid down by our Lord, "By their fruits shall ye know them". The Gospel of Christ is to be reflected in the Christian character. Herein lies the answer to those who misrepresent the Gospel, i.e. the antinomians. "To this present hour the same objections are made to all those statements which

[1] Sermon 2365 (on James 2.24)—"Justification by Works."
[2] Sermon 1457—"Self-Confidence Condemned."   [3] Sermon 709.

resemble Paul's. If we deny to good works the office of justifying the soul, we are represented as denying the necessity of them altogether. Though these objections have been refuted a thousand times and should be refuted ten thousand times more, the enemies of the Gospel will still repeat them with as much confidence as ever." He adds: it is curious that "the very persons who are complained of for the licentious tendency of their principles, should at the same time be universally condemned for the over-righteous sanctity of their lives". He also reproves those "who are so occupied with contemplating what Christ has wrought out *for* them, that they cannot bestow a thought on what he has engaged to work *in* them. To speak of holiness, or any point of duty, they account low and legal; yea, they think that Christ has by his own obedience to the law superseded the necessity of holiness in us; and that the whole work of salvation is so finished by him, that there remains nothing to be done by us, nothing of repentance for sin, nothing of obedience to God's commandments, but solely to maintain confidence in the provisions of God's everlasting covenant and to rejoice in God as our God and portion". Simeon will have none of this, and he warns the young in the audience that they cannot honour Christ by setting aside any of his commands.

Simeon took no narrow view of salvation, for he saw the outreach of the Gospel not only to the whole world but into society itself. That is why he showed so great an interest in India, the Church Missionary Society, the Jews, the Bible Society, and other causes. He played a full part in public affairs in addition to his primary ministry among individuals as an evangelist and director. He was deeply concerned that the poor in Cambridge should be able to get cheap bread, and during the great scarcity of 1788 he himself rode out to the surrounding villages every Monday to see that the bakers did their duty and sold to the poor at half price, the other half being paid by public subscription to which he contributed very generously.[1] It is not within the scope of this essay to examine Simeon's philanthropy or his attitude to foreign missions, but it is not out of place to suggest that these are corollaries to his understanding of the Gospel of salvation. He would not have found it possible to divorce the Gospel from social responsibility as it was understood by the men of his day, even

[1] Carus, pp. 8of.

though he never asked the kind of questions that were later to be raised by F. D. Maurice and others. But Simeon did not have an enquiring and restless mind. He was a man of action; he had a ministerial priesthood of ever-widening influence to exercise; others could ask questions, he would get on with the job.

It is interesting to notice three points about Simeon's view of conversion.

1. Despite his preaching for decision in apostolic style he admitted that he was unable to specify *the day* of his conversion, though he knew the *season*, Lent and Passiontide, 1779.[1]

2. He did not accept the doctrine of total depravity in the strict Calvinist sense, and so he could write "The unconverted are justly offended when we represent the natural man as destitute of any kind of good; and the godly are discouraged when we represent them as having in them no remnant of evil". Simeon was too much of a realist—and too observant—to hold either of these positions. "We may in a general way represent both of them as resembling a river where the tide flows: the natural man as descending from the fountain-head to the ocean; and the spiritual man as returning with equal force to the fountain-head."[2] He makes another of his subtle distinctions at this point. "Towards *God*, I grant, our fallen nature retains not even the smallest measure of that love, which at our first creation filled our souls. . . . But *all* good is not so obliterated, but there may be found in many unconverted men as fixed a principle of truth and benevolence, and honour and integrity as in the generality of true Christians: and if we so state our views of the fall as to rob the whole mass of mankind of this honour, we cast a stumbling-block in their way, and excite a very bitter prejudice against the Gospel. On the other hand, if we represent the work of grace as so entire, that there remains no corruption in the persons who experience it, we reduce even the most eminent Christians to despair."[3] We may notice again how Simeon approaches this problem primarily as a pastor, concerned with the *effect* of a particular doctrine both on the converted and the unconverted. Just as the attitude of a medical man may be expected to change when he leaves the laboratory for the clinic, so that of the Christian minister may

---

[1] Carus, pp. 710f.
[2] Letter to the Rev. John Venn, Carus, p. 790.   [3] Carus, p. 791.

moderate when he leaves purely academic theology for the day-to-day encounter with men and women in different states of need for whom theology has to be made relevant.

3. The agent of conversion and all that follows it by way of change of character is the Holy Spirit. Simeon compares the Spirit's power of attraction to the influence of the moon upon the tide. "It is generally acknowledged that the tide is effected by the moon. This to a person uninformed upon the subject would appear a downright absurdity: for, as he knows not the powers of attraction, he cannot conceive how it should be possible for the moon to possess an influence which not all the human race combined would be able to exert. But experience shows that, whether we can comprehend it or not, the ocean does obey the influence of the moon. In like manner the change wrought in the heart of man depends altogether on the influence of the Holy Spirit; and however incapable we may be of comprehending the Spirit's operations, we must refer to Him the entire change which is wrought in us in the conversion of our souls to God."[1] But even the Holy Spirit does not override the power of human volition, for "the ungodly are voluntary agents in all that they do, and the godly also are perfectly voluntary in their motions". The Spirit draws them "not as mere machines, but 'with the cords of a man and with the bands of love' ".[2]

* * *

By implication we have already noticed some of Simeon's emphases about the Christian life itself, and it will have become clear that he was strongly opposed to any kind of perfectionist doctrine. This was his chief criticism of the Methodists. "Of that body there are many thousands, I doubt not, who are truly and eminently pious; but there are also many who are lamentably enthusiastic and deluded. The doctrine of sinless perfection is not only espoused by many of them, but maintained as actually existing in their own experience." Happening to meet a large party of people in Carlisle who held these views, Simeon tried to show them what he conceived to be "the evil with which these sentiments were pregnant". He made the following six points:

1. They lead persons to look for perfection in themselves instead of searching out their imperfections.

[1] Carus, p. 792.   [2] Cf. p. 79 above.

2. They lead persons to wink hard at their own imperfections, and even their sins, and to call them only temptations, which they consider as no sins.

3. They fill with undue self-complacency those who fancy that they have attained perfection.

4. They prevent those persons from humbling themselves in prayer before God as they ought, and lead them to abound rather in Pharisaical thanksgivings; "I thank Thee, etc."

5. They discourage exceedingly those who cannot find in themselves such attainments.

6. They generate the wildest notions imaginable, namely, that men are perfected at this or that instant; when the whole Scripture speaks of sanctification as gradual and progressive.[1]

"I love and honour Wesley", said Simeon one Friday evening, "yet the Wesleyans are under a delusion as to perfection. The Scripture word *perfect* (teleios) is the idea of full growth, and not their view. I once heard a man say in the presence of Wesley and others, 'I have known God for thirty-six years: for twenty-eight years I have never known an evil thought, and have loved the Lord with all my heart, and soul, and mind, and strength.' Another man acknowledged himself (like me) a sinner; but Wesley and all the rest praised the former man. I said it was delusion; but it was not my place to argue there and then."[2] Simeon had too much common sense, even as a young man as he must have been on this occasion, to be taken in by any boasts about sinlessness.

Commenting on the text "Whosoever is born of God doth not commit sin; for his seed remaineth in him: and he cannot sin, because he is born of God" (1 John 3.9), he says: "He is not a worker of sin, not an habitual sinner of any kind. The grace which is in him opposes sin: it may decay, may be overcome, may be lost, but it is resolutely opposed to any evil habit or any wilful sin. The man cannot live in the habit of sinning. . . . It is an error to refer this passage to sinless perfection, as the Wesleyans do; or to an indefectible principle of grace, as the Calvinists do. . . ."[3]

Simeon preferred to think of the Christian life in terms of brokenness. Again and again he reverts to this idea, particularly

[1] Carus, p. 161.   [2] Brown, p. 225.   [3] Brown, p. 103.

in his latter years. In a diary of a journey to Paris he records a conversation with the Duchess de Broglie,[1] whom he describes as "a lovely woman and very sensible". She had a strong aversion to Calvinism and a strong conviction that the heathen would be saved, "because it would be contrary to all that God has done for the salvation of the world, to punish those to whom that salvation has not been revealed". So Simeon expounded to her his own views of Scripture, and "I shewed her that brokenness of heart was the key to the whole".[2] On another occasion when he was asked what he considered to be the mark of regeneration he replied: "The very first and indispensable sign is self-loathing and abhorrence. Nothing short of this can be admitted as an evidence of a real change. . . . I have constantly pressed this subject upon my congregation, and it has been the characteristic of my ministry. I want to see more of this humble, contrite, broken spirit among us."[3] Writing in 1832 to Daniel Wilson, Bishop of Calcutta, he said: "Repentance is in every view so desirable, so necessary, so suited to honour God, that I seek *that* above all. The tender heart, the broken and contrite spirit, are to me far above all the joys that I could ever hope for in this vale of tears. I long to be in my proper place, my hand on my mouth, and my mouth in the dust. I would rather have my seed-time here, and wait for my harvest till I myself am carried to the granary of heaven. I feel this to be safe ground. Here I cannot err. If I have erred all my days, I cannot err here. I am sure that whatever God may despise (and I fear that there is much which passes under the notion of religious experience that will not stand very high in his estimation), He will not despise the broken and contrite heart. I love the picture of the heavenly hosts, both saints and angels: all of them are upon their faces before the throne. . . . But I am running on farther than I like to do on such *interior* subjects. . . ."[4] Almost at the end of his life and after recovering from illness he wrote in another letter: "I am sorry to hear that your eyes are weak; and I earnestly hope that the relaxation from their wonted labours for the body will be improved by turning them in more steadily upon the inward man, and fixing them more intently on Him who died for us upon the cross, and ever lives to make intercession for us at the right hand of God. Standing as I

---

[1] Daughter of Madame de Staël.
[2] Carus, p. 580.   [3] Carus, p. 650.   [4] Carus, pp. 695f.

do on the very brink and precipice of the eternal world, I desire nothing so much as a broken and contrite spirit."[1]

If we ask how Simeon's intense spirituality grew, the answer lies in his unfailing spiritual discipline. He got up at four o'clock every morning, winter and summer, and spent the first four hours of the day in private prayer and devotional Bible study. He kept no account of these times; we must therefore be content with knowing only the fact. Prayer and Bible study as means of grace ranked very high in his prescription for progress in the Christian life.

He also taught the importance of fasting, holding it to be of great value, "too much thought of among Papists, too little among us. The Gospel contains permission to fast and supposes fasting as a usual habit." In one of his Friday evening parties in 1827 Simeon admitted that he used to fast but did so no longer on health grounds. He was cautious about recommending fasting in his public ministry because "it is so easy to wound weak consciences, or to impose oppressive duties and observance, which shall perhaps turn to bondage. Still, in cases of deep distress, or of deadness of spirit, or of the hidings of God's countenance, or of peculiar temptations, fasting is of great value, and especially in the latter case, for the Lord said of the evil spirit, 'This kind goeth not out but by fasting and prayer'. God's commandments to Christians, in regard of external observances, are general, and not so specific as among the Jews, lest the Christian might fulfil them in the spirit of self-righteousness, and say, I have done all that was required of me by God".[2]

Both by example and precept Simeon stressed almsgiving. In answer to a question about the stewardship of money he gave some quaint details about his own habits in this respect. "When I first came up as an undergraduate, with very scanty means, I made my resolution (and have been enabled to keep it ever since) to show economy to myself, liberality to my friends, generosity to the poor. . . . When an undergraduate, I drank small beer, and gave my ale to the Lord, and this day I did the same, feeling that I did not require ale to-day, and so saved a penny for the Lord. In putting tea into my tea-pot, I have by habit learned to guess the value of even a halfpenny, and when I can, to save it for God. But do not mistake me: this only regards myself personally. I

[1] Carus, p. 716.   [2] Brown, pp. 87ff.

never count pence when my friends are near me. . . . And even as to myself, when sick, I put myself at the head of my own poors' list. . . . I have always given at the beginning of the year a proportion of my goods for God. This share is not mine, and all I have to do with it is to use a rigid economy and judgment in distributing it. I feel myself a steward in all I have, and thus secure a proportion for God. I do not feel I am *giving* it. And whatever I can by economy save for God is in addition to that share. . . . If at the end of the year I have wine etc. in store toward the next year, I have been in the habit of buying it of myself, and giving the purchase money to God, as so much saved for Him. I had rather *save* a penny for God, than *beg* a shilling for Him, and yet you will bear me witness I am a great beggar. Yet there is a proper limit, and circumstances should all be weighed. To rob one's wife and children, and be niggardly to them for the sake of the poor, is not right. That is not self-denial. To rob one's friends of just hospitality for the sake of the poor, or to rob the poor for the sake of hospitality, are neither of them right. I should act very differently, had I a family, from what I now do. . . . If a man has a small income and a large family, so that all his means are absorbed in necessaries for his family, doubtless, God will not refuse to accept his using it all for his family; yet there is a great gratification in giving to God. . . . Observe the blessing promised to liberality: 'He that giveth to the poor, lendeth to the Lord, and look, what he layeth out shall be repaid him.' A High Calvinist wishes such passages were not in Scripture. Yet Christ accepts as done to Himself whatever is done to the poor for His sake. . . . When you give charity, always remember first to give your own selves to God."[1]

Simeon laid great stress on personal holiness, though it was to be pursued by discipline and penitence. "Holiness is a conformity of heart and life to the revealed will of God. . . . Sanctification is a progressive work. A child of God arrives not at full stature but by degrees: he is constantly growing in grace: the vernal bloom gradually advances to the autumnal fruit. There may indeed be seasons wherein he may appear to decline, or may really suffer a declension: but if he have the grace of God in his heart, he will revive, and return to God with more fervour and stedfastness.

[1] Brown, pp. 122–6. I have quoted this at length as an illustration of Simeon's pastoral wisdom.

Nor will he ever think he has already attained, or is already perfect; but 'forgetting the things that are behind, he will reach forward unto that which is before'."[1] Furthermore, "a progress in holiness is above all things to be desired". It comes about through an unalterable determination of the will and the most ardent exercise of the affections. "This is holiness; but nothing short of it will suffice. We do not say that the Christian must be *perfect*: for where should we then find a Christian? but he must aim at perfection, and be continually pressing forwards for the attainment of it."[2]

In connection with the doctrine of sanctification Simeon makes a very shrewd observation. "Religion does not so alter the character as to leave nothing remaining. An ardent and enthusiastic man, when he becomes religious, will still be of the same temperament, and will fail to weigh well various or conflicting duties. . . . But the timid will be timid still; the person who shuddered at a toad before his conversion, will do the same afterwards. Religion gives, indeed, a new direction and tone to the mind. We are vessels, and religion, when poured into us, will taste (as Horace would express it) of the *tan* of the *wood* of our natural dispositions, except in doing away with what is evil and vicious. It will eventually and gradually correct our natural failings, but will not obliterate the effects of nervous or constitutional infirmity."[3]

At this point we may turn to consider Simeon as a spiritual director, concerned with helping people to live the Christian life. The material for this is to be found chiefly in his correspondence. Writing to a young minister who was encountering great difficulties, he pointed him to the Cross. "It is our great aversion to the Cross that makes it burdensome: when we have learned to glory in it, we have found the philosopher's stone. . . . Christ's example alone were enough to animate us; but we have more, incomparably more. All our hopes of salvation are founded, if I may say so, on this: all our prospects of usefulness in the ministry depend on this: all the comfort of our souls in this life is intimately connected with this: that is to say, we cannot hope to enjoy present or future happiness, unless we 'give ourselves

---

[1] Sermon 2337—"The Necessity of Holiness."
[2] Sermon 256—"Disbanding of the Troops of Israel."
[3] Brown, p. 266.

wholly to these things', and 'study to approve ourselves unto God
as workmen that need not to be ashamed'."[1]

To a missionary he writes frankly in reply to a letter which
had indicated some growth in self-knowledge for which Simeon
had been waiting. "You have always appeared to me to be sincere.
But your views of Christianity seemed to be essentially defective.
You have always appeared to admire Christianity *as a system*; but
you never seemed to have just views of Christianity *as a remedy*;
you never seemed to possess self-knowledge, or to know the evil
of your own heart. I never saw you in any deep contrition, much
less anything of a tender self-loathing and self-abhorrence. This
always made me jealous over you with a godly jealousy; and never
till this moment have I had my fears for your ultimate state
removed. . . . You now begin to feel the burthen of sin: you now
begin, though still in a very small degree, to have your mind open
to the corruptions of the heart, and to your need of a dying
Saviour to atone for you by His blood, and a living Saviour to
renew you by the influence of His Spirit. Seek, my dear friend,
to grow in this knowledge; for it is this that will endear the
Saviour to you, and make you stedfast in your walk with God.
This is the foundation which must be dug deep, if you would
ever build high, and the ballast which alone will enable you to
sail."[2]

In the case of a morbid and over-scrupulous young man,
Simeon wrote to his anxious father, the Earl of Harrowby: "My
wish is, that your son should see religion in a cheerful dress; but
that he should never be led to conceive of it as separable, even for
a moment, from wisdom and gravity, from modesty and sobriety." He had instructed a mutual friend "to tell your son from
me, that I thought an hour in the morning, and the same in the
evening, was sufficient for religious exercises, and better than a
longer time".[3] A little later in the same year, 1823, he wrote
further: "Your son wants to *know* whether his heart is right with
God: and through Mr. Elliott (his tutor) I should have led him
insensibly to the knowledge of it, just as I should show a mower
whether he had a proper edge upon his scythe. When he put it in
motion and saw the effects produced, he would have a demonstration which he could not withstand. So your son, brought to
interest himself in works of benevolence abroad, would have his

[1] Carus, pp. 191f.   [2] Carus, pp. 569f.   [3] Carus, pp. 577f.

morbid feelings dispelled; and *his experience* would refute *his arguments*: he would see that he *is* right, in spite of all that a distorted imagination can suggest." Simeon, in another letter to the Earl of Harrowby, recounts how he actually dealt with his troubled son. He said in effect: "Your views of yourself (your own sinfulness), though they may be erroneous, are not one atom too strong. Your sinfulness far exceeds all that you have stated or have any conception of—'your heart is deceitful above all things and desperately wicked: who can know it?' But I have an effectual remedy for them—'The blood of Jesus Christ cleanseth from *all* sin'. I grant that you are lost and utterly undone. So are all mankind—some for gross sins, some for impenitence, some for unbelief, some for pride and self-righteousness, some for other sins. You are lost for the very sins you mention, hardness of heart, indifference, etc. Tell me how are those others to obtain remission? And now tell me where *your* sins are excepted? Tell me where the Lord Jesus Christ has acknowledged himself unable, or declared himself unwilling, to forgive your sins, or to supply the very defects of which you complain. . . . Take a book as large as any in the Bank of England, put down all the sins of which either conscience or morbid imagination accuse you. Fear not to add to their number all that Satan himself can suggest. And this *I* will do—I will put on the Creditor side 'the unsearchable riches of Christ' and will leave you to draw the balance. . . . After you have filled the whole book you will only be humbled more and feel the greater need of a Saviour. You will be necessitated to exalt the Saviour's mercy and love to the utmost as indeed you ought to do. If in this way you obtain peace, the Saviour will be magnified by you: and, the grounds of your peace being in him and not in yourself, it will be subject to no diminution from renewed or even deeper views of your own unworthiness. In this way you will be more and more abased and the Saviour will be more and more exalted as long as you live."[1]

Simeon was able to rebuke when necessary. He writes to a friend to say how grieved he is "to behold with what acrimonious feelings you speak of a variety of persons, whose praise is in all the Churches. Do you not remember what St James says, 'Speak

[1] These last two unpublished letters are in the collection of Harrowby MSS., and it was by the kindness of the present Earl of Harrowby that I was allowed to see them.

not evil one of another, brethren. He that speaketh evil of his brother, and judgeth his brother, speaketh evil of the law, and judgeth the law; but if thou judge the law, thou art not a doer of the law, but a judge. There is one law-giver who is able to save and to destroy. Who art thou that judgest another?' St Paul, when he was constrained to condemn what was notoriously evil, said, 'I now tell you even *weeping*'. But you, my dear friend, speak with a degree of malignity that involves your own soul in a greater degree of guilt than that which you condemn in others. Against the Methodists you have taken up a very unwarrantable prejudice. Need you be reminded at this day, that if we have not charity, whatever we may do or suffer for the Lord, we are only 'as sounding brass or tinkling cymbal'. . . . I do indeed make great allowances for you; for it is not easy for a person, noticed and caressed as you are, to preserve an humble spirit. . . . You speak of your having got views of prophecy relating to the second Advent; and you tell us that you are unfolding *them* to your hearers. But I wish you to remember what was the exclusive subject of St Paul's ministry. 'He determined to know nothing amongst his hearers but Jesus Christ, and him *crucified*.' N.B. Not Jesus Christ, and him *reigning* on earth, but Jesus Christ, and him *crucified*. . . . Write me word that you take these suggestions kindly and thankfully at my hands. Write me word that you have spread the matter before the Lord in prayer, and that He has discovered to you your error in indulging so uncharitable a spirit. And then I shall bless God that I have taken up my pen to speak, at the risk of being accounted 'an enemy for telling you the truth'."[1] It should be noticed that all Simeon's admonition is based on Scripture, and as a faithful director he does not shrink from the utmost candour.

To a woman undergoing religious depression he wrote that he would have preferred half an hour's conversation to a thousand letters, and then he turned to her need. "Your case in few words is this: 'I was once in earnest about my soul: I have since declined: I feel but cold at this moment and unhumbled, whilst confessing what ought to humble me in the dust. What must I do to get myself quickened in the divine life, and stimulated to run the race set before me?' " Simeon tells her to read the Scriptures and to be much in prayer and meditation, relying on Christ and his promises.

[1] Carus, pp. 628f.

He then adds: "There are two errors which are common to persons in your state; First, the using of means, as though by the use of them they could prevail; and secondly, the not using them, because they have so long been used in vain. The error consists in putting the means too much in the place of Christ, and in expecting from *exertion* what is only gained by *affiance*. . . . The willingness to be saved by him altogether from first to last, and in his own time and way, and this determination to trust in him though he slay you, and to praise him though he condemn you, is what you particularly want. You would fain have the *knowledge* of your acceptance of him, when you should rather be concerned to *insure* that acceptance."[1]

It should be clear from this selection of quotations that Simeon was a spiritual director of great insight and sympathy. He never under-estimated the difficulties of the Christian life nor the Christian's need for counsel and encouragement. He had an extraordinary wisdom in much of the advice he gave—in this, for instance: "In matters of conscience, the first thoughts are always sure to be the correct ones; second thoughts are sure to be contaminated with motive and policy. In matters of policy, however, second thoughts are generally the soundest."[2] His attitude to the world was broader than one would have imagined from a merely superficial acquaintance with his works. Thus, he did not regard dancing as a sin *per se*, nor cards. "If I had an aged parent, or a sick and languid relative, unable to bear much conversation or reading or solitude, and I was to engage with him or her in a game of piquet, would it be wrong? No, it would be a harmless recreation, and useful. But I would never make a fourth at a party of whist nor introduce cards among friends at my own house, nor enter into them elsewhere." As for dancing, he would dance with children and feel that private dancing in the family circle was allowable. He strongly recommended recreation, particularly tennis and riding, for keeping fit. "Serve God in your recreations and enjoy Him; but we are too often like the Jews or like the monks, afraid of God's blessings. We have the spirit of 'Touch not, taste not', but this is wrong. 'God giveth us richly all things to enjoy,' and we ought to enjoy God in everything; to feel the delight of affluence, science, friends, recreations, children, in fact of everything, as coming to us from God, who gives its sweetness, and for

[1] Carus, pp. 733f. [2] Brown, p. 266.

whose sake and glory it is."[1] Simeon had a thoroughly positive attitude to the Christian life, even in days when there were more scruples about amusements than there generally are to-day.

* * *

It is almost commonplace to say that Simeon was a strong churchman. He and other leading Evangelicals deeply revered the two great Sacraments of the Gospel; they regarded them as means of grace but denied that they had any saving effect.[2] Evangelicals believed that salvation comes as God's unmerited gift in Christ and that it is received through personal faith in Him and not through *doing* anything. Simeon was concerned to expound a Prayer Book view of both Sacraments, stressing their importance and efficacy, but to steer clear of any suggestion that the Sacraments alone, as outward acts, could save a man. They were means of grace but not necessarily in themselves means of salvation. "I would on no account depreciate baptism, or detract from its importance. It is necessary for all who embrace the faith of Christ: and is replete with blessings to all who receive it aright. Even the outward ministry of it gives us a *title* to the blessings of the Christian covenant. . . . But if we receive it not aright, we are still like Simon Magus 'in the gall of bitterness and the bond of iniquity'. To receive any *saving* benefit (for if it be rightly received, 'baptism doth save us' [1 Peter 3.21]) we must have not only the *sign* but *the thing signified*", i.e. baptism with the Holy Ghost and fire, death to sin, new birth to righteousness.[3] This represents Simeon's fundamental distinction which he insists on repeatedly in his discussions on this subject, on which Evangelicals have often seemed to be rather uneasy because of their emphasis upon personal conversion and justification by faith. It may be claimed that Simeon makes an honest attempt to surmount these difficulties and to sort them out. Unfortunately there is no single treatise in which he sets forth his views on Baptism; they have to be culled from a variety of sources, mostly his sermons. We will select some of the points he makes.

1. He accepted the traditional view that the ark was typical of the Church of Christ. As Noah was saved by admission into it,

[1] Brown, pp. 246, 247, 251f.
[2] G. W. E. Russell, *A Short History of the Evangelical Movement*, 1915, p. 12.
[3] Sermon 1283—"The Baptism of the Spirit."

so are we by introduction, i.e. Baptism, into the Church. The ark was wisely framed. It "did not accord with those principles of navigation which obtain amongst us: it was defective in some of the most essential points; it had no mast, no sails, no rudder. . . . The Church too is constituted far otherwise than human wisdom would have framed it. Man would have left room for the display of his own skill, and for the establishment of his own righteousness". We, like Noah, are to use the appointed means of salvation, to enter into the ark. And it is Christ who says, "I am the door". Some will say, We are in the ark already. To this objection Simeon replies: "It is granted that as far as the ark depicts the *visible* Church of Christ, we are all inclosed in it. [A foot-note explains that baptism admits us into the ark of Christ's Church.] But we must distinguish between the visible and the invisible Church. Our blessed Lord has taught us to distinguish between the fruitful and the unfruitful branches, which, though they are both 'in Him', will be very differently dealt with by the great Husbandman." He also quotes the parables of the drag-net and the tares as well as St Paul's attitude to "Israel after the flesh". "Let us not then deceive ourselves, or imagine that we must of necessity be saved because we have been baptized: for there was an accursed Ham in the ark, as well as a righteous Noah: but let us inquire into the dispositions and habits of our minds. . . . It is not any outward privilege or profession that constitutes us Christians, but an inward change of heart."[1] Here again we find the distinction between outward and inward, the sign and the thing signified, being pressed home. Elsewhere he compares too great a stress on the outward act of Baptism *per se* to the teaching of the Judaizing Christians in the early Church. "Some, and some of no mean name, have gone so far as to assert that the very act of Baptism saves us. . . . It seems incredible that such Jewish blindness should exist at this day in the Christian Church. Others, even the great mass of nominal Christians, imagine that the attending of the house of God and the Lord's Supper, together with common honesty, is sufficient to procure us acceptance with God; or that if a little more be wanting the merits of Christ will turn the scale."[2]

At the same time Simeon is ready to admit that Baptism, though not necessarily accompanied by "the washing away of sin" (e.g.

[1] Sermon 16—"The Preservation of Noah."
[2] Sermon 1783—"The Ceremonial Law Abrogated."

in the case of Simon Magus) was ordinarily and intimately connected with it (e.g. in the case of Saul of Tarsus, who could only enter the Church through the rite of Baptism). "Of itself, indeed, it could do nothing; but as used in faith, it did much. As appointed of God, it was a sign of the person's believing in Christ, and a seal of the righteousness which he had received through faith. It was also an acknowledgment on the sinner's part that he was bound to serve the Lord in the way of holiness; and a pledge on God's part that he should have grace and strength to do so, if only he would seek it in the exercise of faith and prayer. Thus it was intimately connected both with the justification of the soul and its sanctification after the divine image. . . . As enjoined of God, the rite is *necessary* for all, but as performed by man it is effectual to those only who receive it aright." [1]

2. Simeon is completely happy about the Prayer Book services of Baptism and their references to regeneration. "St Paul says that *all* who have been baptized have put on Christ—not some or many or most." But he was speaking here according to the judgement of charity, even as he does in many other places where he addresses whole collective bodies and Churches as "saints and faithful in the Lord". "And I cannot but think that in this passage we have a complete justification of the language used by our reformers in the baptismal service." Admittedly the language is strong, "but is it stronger than the Apostle's language in my text?" If we don't complain of Paul's language, we must not complain of the reformers'.

Simeon thinks of Baptism as something objective, but objective in a covenant sense and therefore not unconditional. In his jubilee sermon after fifty years as minister of Holy Trinity, Cambridge, he reminds his congregation of their Baptism. "There Christ was received by you as your Lord and Saviour, and you professed to look for remission of sins altogether in His name and through faith in his blood and righteousness. At the same time you gave up yourselves to him to be sanctified in body, soul and spirit by his grace, and to live altogether to his glory. But if you recede in any respect from these engagements . . . you forfeit that remission, which, if you received your baptism aright, or subsequently realized the engagements there entered into, was conceded to you." [2]

[1] Sermon 1806—"The Conversion of St Paul."
[2] Sermon 2421—"A Pastoral Admonition."

Yet Simeon urges that Baptism and regeneration must not be confused. He admits that in the early Church the two terms were virtually synonymous because "none but truly regenerate persons would submit to a rite which engaged them to separate themselves from an ungodly world". But there is a wide difference between the two. Regeneration is absolutely necessary for salvation, whereas Baptism could be dispensed with "under some circumstances", e.g. the penitent thief. "Baptism is an outward work of man upon the body; regeneration is an inward work of God upon the soul. . . . Our faculties indeed remain the same as they were before; but there is a new direction given to them all."[1]

Simeon's most elaborate treatment of this theme comes in the third of a course of four university sermons entitled "An Appeal to Men of Wisdom and Candour", in which he sets out his views on certain cardinal doctrines under discussion, showing that revealed religion, though not founded on reason nor making appeal to it, "yet is perfectly consistent with reason and approves itself to the judgment of everyone whose mind is enlightened by the Spirit of God". This particular sermon is on the New Birth.[2] It begins with a disclaimer, saying what new birth does not mean. "It is supposed by men . . . that we require a *sudden* impulse of the Spirit, which, *without any co-operation on the part of man*, is to convert the soul to God; and that we require this change to be so sensibly and perceptibly wrought, that the subject of it shall be able to specify the day and hour when it took place." But Simeon means no such thing. Acknowledging that God may work this way, as at Pentecost and with Saul, he adds: "But we require nothing *sudden*. It may be so gradual, as that the growth of it, like the seed in the parable, shall at no time be particularly visible, either to the observation of others, or to the person's own mind. . . . We deny that we ever speak of it as wrought by an irresistible impulse of the Spirit, or without the co-operation of the man himself: for that man is in all cases a free agent: he is never wrought upon as a mere machine. . . . How far the Spirit of God works, and how far the mind of man, is a point which no human being can determine." But this change in a man is not to be identified with baptism, otherwise "Why should our Lord . . . so carefully distinguish between water-baptism and the operations

---

[1] Sermon 1608—"The Nature and Necessity of Regeneration."
[2] Sermon 1975.

of the Holy Spirit?" In the discourse with Nicodemus our Lord compares one born of the Spirit to the wind blowing where it listeth. But Baptism has no connection with wind, argues Simeon. "It were much to be wished, that those who will have baptism to be the new birth would take this passage and try what sense they can make of it according to their interpretation. . . . If by the term regeneration they meant an introduction into a new *state*, in which the baptized persons have a right and a title to all the blessings of salvation, we should have no controversy with them. If they meant that all adults, who in the exercise of penitence and faith are baptized into Christ, have in that ordinance the remission of their sins sealed to them, and the Holy Spirit in a more abundant measure communicated to them, we should not disagree with them. If they meant that infants dedicated to God in baptism may and sometimes *do* (though in a way not discoverable to us, except by the fruits) receive a new nature from the Spirit of God *in*, and *with*, and *by* that ordinance, we should cordially join with them. But they go much further than all this; and assert that *all persons* do *necessarily* by a divine appointment receive the Holy Ghost in such a manner and degree as really to be changed in the spirit of their minds into the very image of God in righteousness and true holiness, and so to partake of the divine nature that they never need afterwards to seek so great a change again. *This* we are constrained to combat as a fundamental error."

We can see what Simeon is anxious to preserve—the morality of the sacraments. The doctrine of Baptism which he is criticizing "tends to lull men asleep in their evil ways, to make them think that they do not need a new nature, but only a little reform of some things which may easily be amended whenever they please". He will not allow that Baptism "works" irrespective of the response of faith at some time or other. He will not allow that Baptism makes a subsequent repentance and conversion experience unnecessary or superfluous. "The chief source of error is failure to distinguish between a change of *state* and a change of *nature*. Baptism is change of state, entitling us to blessings of the new covenant. It is not change of nature, though this may be communicated at the time the ordinance is administered." Simeon stuck loyally to the Prayer Book forms but he felt that "had the Reformers lived now they might have varied the words and the form a little. . . . The word 'regeneration', in our present use, is a novel word. It is only twice used in Scripture (Matt. 19.28, Titus 3.5), and in neither passage does it mean what we now mean by the new birth. Nor does Beza, nor any other early Reformer, ever use it to signify what we mean by the new birth. St Paul uses it, and the early Reformers use it, for mere baptism. And the modern sense, which it has acquired in the last century or half century, is not that in which it was used when the Prayer Book was drawn up. It was not then as now synonymous with what we mean by the new birth, the entire change of soul. . . . The early Reformers used the word 'regeneration' as meaning baptism, which changes our state; not conversion, which changes our nature; or, at least, they use it for the beginning of that process by which we are changed, and not the change as if effected at once".[1] This is a very important passage, for it shows how earnestly Simeon attempted to bring some kind of common usage into the confusion of Evangelical vocabulary, which still lingers on. Simeon is perfectly happy about the phrase "baptismal regeneration", provided regeneration is not identified with conversion. He argues that the Prayer Book forms are entirely consonant with Scriptural language and that none of the phrases used about the child's regeneration are too strong. The difficulty had arisen through the recent non-scriptural use of the word "regeneration" as synonymous with the experience of new birth or new nature in a moral sense, which had come to so many during the Evangelical Revival. "The Reformers could never mean that Baptism, and what *we* now understand by the new birth, or new nature, were the same, for facts prove the contrary."[2]

3. On the basis of this distinction between a new state and a new nature, or between regeneration and conversion, Simeon could defend the practice of infant baptism without the least hesitation and criticize the Baptists in doing so. Baptism is the means of admission into the religion of the new covenant, superseding circumcision which admitted children into the old covenant when only eight days old. "If God has not deprived children of being admitted into covenant with him, who are we, that we should take it from them? By thus robbing them of their privileges, we represent Jesus Christ as less merciful to children now, than he was to the children of Jewish parents." Moreover, the command to circumcise children on the eighth day "sufficiently

---

[1] Brown, pp. 232–4.   [2] Brown, p. 230.

shows that the children who died under that age, did not perish for the mere want of that ordinance: and Christian parents may be equally assured, that if their infants die before they have been initiated into the Christian covenant by baptism, the want of that ordinance will not affect their eternal welfare".[1]

About Confirmation Simeon does not have anything of special significance to say. It was not then a controversial subject. He thought it to be "highly valuable as giving a minister contact with his flock; as opening their minds, at a peculiar season of life, and with the power of specific duty, to instructions which else would come sleepily upon them". He noted in 1828 that the new Bishop of London, Dr Blomfield, was about to make confirmations annual and the parties of catechumens small. Simeon was very pleased about this and felt it would cause confirmation to be much more what it was designed to be.[2] In a sermon on vows[3] he makes explicit reference to Confirmation as the renewal of baptismal vows, drawing a parallel with the presentation of Jewish children in the Temple at twelve years old, "that they might come more fully under the yoke of the law. . . . So among us, at a somewhat later age, are young people called upon to present themselves unto the Lord, and to take upon themselves those engagements which were made for them at their baptism by their sponsors". He gave his ordinands careful instruction in how to prepare candidates for confirmation, and he warned sponsors of their great responsibilities, for "the ordinance of confirmation as administered in the Established Church, is of the utmost importance to be well improved by ministers for the benefit of their flocks, and by young people for the everlasting benefit of their own souls".[4] As we have noted before in connection with other doctrines, Simeon's approach is that of the pastor, concerned with the welfare of his people, not that of the theologian, interested in various points of view.

The doctrine of Holy Communion was not a matter either of controversy or even of discussion to any great extent in Simeon's life-time. There is much evidence that he greatly revered this

[1] Sermon 27—"The Circumcision of Abraham."
[2] Brown, p. 239. Before Bishop Blomfield's time confirmation was administered very infrequently, only once in four or five years.
[3] Sermon 595.
[4] Sermon 1761—"The Ethiopian Eunuch's Confession."

Sacrament and it was through preparing for it in his first year as an undergraduate at King's that he found spiritual peace and entered into the experience of "being saved". But apart from a number of references in his biography about attendance at Holy Communion there is little material to indicate his teaching on this; such as there is comes from a few of the sermons—but only very few. It is probable that Simeon would frequently have read to his congregation the exhortations in the Communion Service and that he would have instructed confirmation candidates in its meaning. He said explicitly: "I always lead the young to view [confirmation] as a preparatory step to Communion rather than as an object in itself."[1] He hopes that the young candidates will soon be "frequent communicants at the Lord's Supper. . . . Your confirmation is intended to be a preparation for that holy ordinance, and it is of no real utility to you, if it be not followed up by a total surrender of yourselves to God at the table of your Lord. Now at the Lord's table we give up ourselves wholly to the Lord. . . . We declare before all, that we are determined, through grace, to live and die in this sacred cause, having no hope but in his atoning blood, no strength but in his grace, no rule but his revealed will, no end of life but the glory of his name".[2]

As Simeon's general preaching was mainly a systematic exposition of Holy Scripture rather than a coverage of doctrines or topical subjects, his only reason for preaching on the Holy Communion would be when it was the subject matter of the passage concerned. The material, therefore, is limited mostly to 1 Corinthians 11 and the dominical institution of the Eucharist at the Last Supper.

This Sacrament was for Simeon primarily a feeding upon Christ. The Passover was a type of the Lord's Supper; both were commemorative of redemption, both were "instructive emblems", and both were feasts. "The killing of the paschal lamb was not sufficient; the people must feed upon it, in the manner which God Himself had prescribed." So must it be with the Lord's Supper. "We must apply it, everyone of us, to ourselves: we must feed upon it; and by so doing declare our affiance in it: we must shew that as our bodies are nourished by bread and wine, so we hope to have our souls nourished by means of union and communion with our blessed and adorable Redeemer. Hence the command

[1] Brown, p. 239.   [2] Sermon 595—"Vows to be Performed."

given to everyone, to eat the bread, and to drink the cup. And a more instructive ordinance cannot be conceived; since it shews, that it is by an actual fellowship with Christ in his death, and by that alone, that we can ever become partakers of the benefits which it has procured for us." Again, "It is a memorial of the death of Christ and a medium of communion with Christ, whose body and blood we feed upon in the sacred elements, and by whom we are strengthened for all holy obedience." It will be seen that this kind of sacramentalism was a useful corrective to the tendency which Simeon had criticized elsewhere of an over-emphasis on "Christ for us" at the expense of a sufficient emphasis on "Christ in us".

This service, says Simeon, is still honoured with Christ's "peculiar presence". He interprets our Lord's words that he would no more drink of the fruit of the wine till he should drink it new with his disciples in the Kingdom of God, as referring to the sacramental life of the Church, for "His Kingdom, properly speaking, is now come"—it has been established through the agency of the Holy Ghost. The renewed manifestations of his presence are to be found in this ordinance, not corporally but spiritually. He comes to us, makes his abode with us, sups with us. It is to be noted in this connection that Simeon interprets Revelation 3.20 and John 14.21,23 eucharistically.

Simeon points out that the first Christians observed the Lord's Supper every day, not only because he commanded it but because of "the blessing which they obtained in the administration of it". He seals it with a peculiar blessing; again and again he "made himself known to them in the breaking of bread"—this was the universal Christian experience. The completion of the Eucharist and its full realization will be in the eternal world, where we shall spiritually renew this feast. "To all eternity will 'this wine be new' to those who drink it; the wonders of redeeming love being more and more unfolded to every admiring and adoring soul."[1]

It is very clear that Simeon taught the importance of regular attendance at Holy Communion and that he strongly disapproved of occasional conformity. "To come to the Lord's table, as many do, at the three great festivals of the Church, and to neglect it all the year besides, is to shew at once that they enter not into the

[1] All these quotations are to be found in Sermon 1401 on St Matthew 26.29.

true spirit of that ordinance. And to attend it as a test for the holding of a public office, is an horrible abuse of it, which, thank God, is now abolished."[1] Neglecting the Lord's Supper "involves us in the deepest guilt"—for rebellion against Christ's explicit command, for ingratitude towards our greatest Benefactor, for contempt of the richest mercies, and for renunciation of our baptismal covenant, which "we ought to renew and confirm at the Lord's table".[2] He warns against unworthy, ignorant, or uncharitable reception,[3] and he stresses the importance of spiritual preparation, regretting that the duty of self-examination was so much neglected and calling for "devoutest meditations: the affections should be engaged to the uttermost". "Your profiting (at the Lord's Supper) will for the most part be proportioned to your preparation."[4] Concerning admission to the Sacrament Simeon says that "the Church of England, in her practice at least, is too lax; whilst those who dissent from her are too rigid. The minute enquiry into what is called *experience* of individuals, and persons sitting in judgement upon it, goes far beyond what is authorized by Scripture. The Apostle says, 'Let a man examine *himself* (not stand up to be examined by *others*) and *so* let him come.' "[5]

Beyond this there is little of significance in Simeon's Eucharistic teaching to which attention need be drawn. He lived and died before the Oxford Movement had become a force to be reckoned with. In this sense and for this reason he may be said to be "the last of the Evangelicals" as they were before the subsequent period of unhappy controversy about this Sacrament, which made many Evangelicals so cautious and negative.

In November 1811 Simeon preached a course of four university sermons on "The Excellence of the Liturgy". It is in these that we can assess his general attitude to worship and his delight in its Anglican forms. These sermons were prompted by a pamphlet written by Dr Marsh, the Lady Margaret Professor, entitled "Inquiry respecting the neglecting to give the Prayer Book with

[1] Sermon 1761—"The Ethiopian Eunuch's Confession."
[2] Sermon 1978, on 1 Corinthians 11.24,26—"The Design and Importance of the Lord's Supper."
[3] Sermon 1979—"On Eating and Drinking Our Own Damnation."
[4] Sermon 1980—"On the Preparation Requisite Before the Lord's Supper."
[5] Sermon 1761—"The Ethiopian Eunuch's Confession."

the Bible", a criticism of the recently formed British and Foreign Bible Society, accusing its promoters not only of Calvinism but also of a loose attachment to the English liturgy. Simeon leapt to their defence.

He chose as his text Deuteronomy 5.28–29: "They have well said all that they have spoken: O that there were such an heart in them!"[1] The context, of course, refers to the fear of the children of Israel before the majesty of the Lord revealed at Mount Sinai. The first sermon is a straightforward exposition and application of the meaning of the passage. The theme is that transient sentiments must be turned into permanent dispositions and not be allowed to disappear when the alarming circumstances which rouse them no longer obtain. There are three such sentiments on which the preacher dwells: an acknowledgment that they could not stand before the divine majesty, a desire for a mediator, and their promise of obedience—all belonging to a proper act of worship.

The other sermons expound the text in "an accommodated sense" with reference to our requests to God in the liturgy of the Established Church, and for our purpose the second is the most important. It is a fine apologia for the very principle of liturgy. Our English Liturgy, says Simeon, "is a composition of unrivalled excellence and needs only the exercise of our devout affections to render it a most acceptable service before God". He proceeds to defend the use of liturgical forms as both lawful and expedient. It is lawful because God prescribed the use of forms of prayer for the Jewish nation (Numbers 6.23–26; 1 Chronicles 16.7–36); the psalms were all used as devotional forms; and Jesus taught a form of prayer. Even those opposed to the liturgy use forms, because hymns are also forms in this sense. "If it be lawful to worship God in forms of verse, is it not equally so in forms of prose?"

But the use of a liturgy is also expedient. This was so at the time of the Reformation and it remains so still. It was expedient at the Reformation because it dispelled ignorance. Without the Book of Common Prayer the people of England would still be in spiritual darkness, but through it "every part of the kingdom became in a good measure irradiated with Scriptural knowledge and with saving truth". It was a standard of piety of inestimable worth,

[1] Sermons 191–4.

and it has served to "perpetuate the flame which the Lord himself, at the time of the Reformation, kindled upon our altars". Turning to the present, the preacher asserts that "to lead the devotions of a congregation in extempore prayer is a work for which but few are qualified". Those ministers who have to lead worship without a suitable form must often wish that they had one. For it secures us against tedious repetitions. Moreover, if anyone finds the liturgy dull and formal, "let him only examine his frame of mind when engaged in extemporaneous prayers, whether in public or in his own family; and he will find that his formality is not confined to the service of the Church, but is the sad fruit and consequence of his own weakness and corruption". Spiritual edification comes from solid truths, not fluent words. It consists in humility of mind and a more holy and consistent walk with God. This is "more valuable than all the animal fervour that ever was excited". The charms of novelty in extempore prayer are delusive, but the prayer of faith, whether with or without form, shall never go forth in vain. "Thousands have found God as present with them in the use of the public services of our Church as ever they did in their secret chambers."

Simeon then turns to deal with certain objections raised against the Prayer Book liturgy. One concerns baptismal regeneration, which we have already discussed above. Another concerns the optimistic assumptions of the Burial Service! Some apparently found difficulty in expressing the sure and certain hope of the resurrection to eternal life over one who had possibly died in his sins. Simeon defends the prayer by pointing out that we speak not of *his* resurrection but of *the* resurrection, adding that we do not absolutely know that God has *not* pardoned a person, and we may certainly hope that he has. St Paul in his epistles often commended all, when in strictness of speech (according to the critics) he should have made some exceptions.

The third sermon extols the excellence of the liturgy. As a result of its successive revisions "it has been brought to such a state of perfection, as no human composition of equal size and variety can pretend to". He draws attention to: (1) Its spirituality and purity: all its services are centred in Christ. (2) Its fullness and suitableness: "there is no possible situation in which we can be placed but the prayers are precisely suited to us; nor can we be in any frame of mind, wherein they will not express our feelings as strongly and forcibly as any person could express them even in his secret chamber". (3) Its moderation and candour: the compilers do not dwell on doctrines after the manner of human systems. But Simeon admits to disliking the damnatory clauses in the Athanasian Creed. "I would rather deplore the curse that awaits them than denounce it, and rather weep over them in my secret chamber than utter anathemas against them in the house of God."[1] With this sole exception, however, Simeon would say that it is not for us to criticize the Liturgy; rather should we let ourselves be cast in its mould. "Let us only suppose that on any particular occasion there were in all of us such a state of mind as the Liturgy is suited to express, what glorious worship would ours be! and how certainly would God delight to hear and bless us." The fourth sermon considers the Ordinal and therefore need not be discussed here. Simeon concludes by urging that no occasion should be given to men to seek for that in other places, which is so richly provided for them in their own Church, and warning the clergy "that the Liturgy itself will appear against us in judgment, if we labour not to the utmost of our power to fulfil the engagements which we have voluntarily entered into".

Perhaps enough has now been said to illustrate the kind of teaching which Simeon gave during his famous ministry of over fifty years. It is all pastoral theology in the sense that it was theology for the congregation rather than the lecture-room. There is nothing original, let alone brilliant, in Simeon's writings. His great achievement was the way in which he interpreted and stated the doctrines of Scripture so as to help men live their Christian life. He did this with independence of mind, shrewdness of judgement, and lucidity of speech and pen. He knew the Bible and he knew the human heart. He steered his own way through the celebrated controversies of his day, accepting and proclaiming the doctrines of predestination and election in moderate language, not because they were in Calvin but because they were in Scripture, teaching and warning his people about apostasy, not because of Arminius and Wesley but because of the New Testament, and because he knew the perils and pitfalls of the Christian pilgrimage. He led men to the knowledge of Jesus Christ as Saviour, because he preached Christ crucified and expounded the meaning of

[1] For a further discussion on the Athanasian Creed, see Brown, p. 142.

justification by faith; but he led them onward to stability and maturity by emphasizing the importance of good works and holding up an ideal of personal holiness. He believed in the objectivity of both the Gospel Sacraments, but he laid stress upon the importance of right reception in the case of both Baptism and the Eucharist, and he distinguished between regeneration and conversion in the case of Baptism. If for no other reason than this, his pastoral theology deserves to be remembered. The language that he sometimes used is of a day that will not return. His preaching belongs wholly to a past which it would be folly to attempt to imitate or reproduce. The controversies of his age have largely disappeared from Anglicanism as we know it now, though in some circles there are occasions when these issues still live. But the standards Simeon set as preacher, pastor, and director, and the fundamental aims and achievements of his remarkable ministry are an abiding challenge; they should inspire not only Evangelicals but the whole Anglican Communion and beyond, so long as the Christian task remains unfinished.

5

SIMEON'S DOCTRINE OF THE CHURCH

MICHAEL WEBSTER

Simeon's Doctrine of the Church

I is widely held that the great discovery of the Church in the twentieth century is itself. In this brief essay it is not possible to discuss the various factors that have made for this re-discovery—the growth of what is called "Biblical theology", the various "movements" of the Church—ecumenical, liturgical, sociological—all influenced by the trend towards a more concrete conception of "community" which is so characteristic of twentieth century thought. In this development of ecclesiology, a great landmark was (we have been recently told by Dr Elliott-Binns[1]) the publication in 1892 of Rudolf Sohm's *Kirchenrecht*, which did not draw the traditional distinction between the Church as a religious concept and as a corporate society. Since the beginning of the century, this idea has been enlarged and developed and, as particularly concerns the Church of England, a great impact was made by the publication in 1936 of the present Archbishop of York's *The Gospel and the Catholic Church*.

Dr Ramsey showed that "Evangelical" and "Catholic" trends in a theology of the Church are both indispensable. "To understand the Catholic Church and its life and order", he wrote, "is to see it as the utterance of the Gospel of God; to understand the Gospel of God is to share with all the saints in the building up of the one Body of Christ . . . hence 'Catholicism' and 'Evangelicalism' are not two separate things which the Church of England must hold together by a great feat of compromise. Rightly understood they are both facts which lie behind the Church of England and, as the New Testament shows, they are one fact . . . the Anglican Church is committed not to a vague position wherein the Evangelical and Catholic views are alternatives but to the scriptural faith wherein both elements are of one."[2]

This concept of the Church has had a profound effect upon a

[1] L. E. Elliott-Binns, *English Thought, 1860–1900, The Theological Aspect*, 1956, p. 263, n. 4.
[2] A. M. Ramsey, *The Gospel and the Catholic Church*, 1936, pp. 208–9.

deeper understanding of some of the doctrines which, at one time, sharply divided the traditional wings of the Anglican Church.[1] It has also had a profound effect upon the life of the Church itself. Writing in 1940, Canon Charles Smyth said that "never in my lifetime have the traditional party divisions in the Church of England been less harmful or more beneficial than in the years preceding the present war".[2] Since the war (and, perhaps, partly because of it) this healing of the divisions has greatly increased so that conventional "party" language tends nowadays to be found more often upon the lips of the older generation. May this be partly due to the fact that the present generation is making an attempt to seize the God-given opportunity to preach not only the doctrines of the Church but the Church itself and, if this be so, that it rightly overwhelms all other things?

But is this "re-discovery" purely and simply a recent development? Were there no prophetic voices in the early nineteenth century that foreshadowed this trend? Indeed there were, and they were heard from both wings of the Church of England. Writing on 11 January 1839 to James Hope-Scott, Gladstone declared: "I am entirely convinced that the movement termed Evangelical and that which is falsely termed Popish are parts of one great beneficent design of God and that, in their substance, they will harmonize and co-operate."[3] On the other side, that great admirer of Simeon, Canon Abner Brown, listened to two sermons preached some years after Simeon's death, one from an Evangelical preacher and the other from one of the Tractarian school. With both of these Brown could heartily concur, feeling that each preacher had taken half of the Scriptural view of the subject and had omitted the other half and that both discourses were needed to exhaust the text.[4] Brown had surely learnt this truth at Simeon's feet. . . . "The truth", wrote Simeon, "is not in the middle and not in one extreme; but in both extremes . . . so

---

[1] For two examples, among (no doubt) many others, see Reinhold Niebuhr, on "The Resurrection of the Body": in *Beyond Tragedy*, 1938, pp. 289–91, and C. F. D. Moule, on "The Eucharistic Sacrifice" in *The Sacrifice of Christ*, 1956, ch. 4.

[2] C. H. E. Smyth, *Simeon and Church Order*, 1940, p. xi.

[3] Quoted by Sir Philip Magnus, *Gladstone*, 1954, p. 35. See also, W. E. Gladstone, *Gleanings of Past Years*, 1879, VII, p. 221. For a critical comment on Gladstone's view, see R. W. Dale, *The Evangelical Revival and other Sermons*, 1880, pp. 2–10.   [4] Brown, pp. 67–8.

that, if extremes please you, I am your man; only remember that it is not to one extreme that we are to go to, but both extremes." [1] With this in mind, Brown wrote that "Mr Simeon's vital Cambridge movement necessitated or at least rendered inevitable the corresponding Oxford Movement of 1832 as to what was sacramental and external." [2]

Because of a general dislike of party patronage trusts in the Church of England, a later age has not entirely appreciated the motives that lay behind Simeon's purchase of livings—they were made with a view to the establishment of a "gospel ministry" and through "love of immortal souls" rather than the manning of citadels against other parties in the Church. [3] Still less acknowledged has been Simeon's care for Church Order, at any rate up to the time of Canon Smyth's Birkbeck lectures of 1937–8. [4] Smyth traces the fascinating battle between Henry Venn and John Berridge showing how Venn was determined to dissuade Simeon from continuing the ecclesiastical irregularities practised by Berridge and how, through a successful outcome of this policy, the Evangelicals were in all probability prevented from leaving the Church of England for dissent or to form a sect of their own. [5] "It was Simeon," says Smyth, "who more than any other single individual taught the younger Evangelicals to love the Church of England and enabled them to feel that they belonged within her body." [6]

In the religious periodicals of his day, Simeon was considered a true churchman—"more of a church-man than a gospel-man". [7] In 1799 it was he who insisted that the new missionary movement was not merged with the London Missionary Society but was called the "Church Missionary Society". [8] When the Bishop of Sodor and Man came to receive communion at Trinity Church, Simeon insisted on administering both elements to him before the remainder of the congregation and justified his action from the Prayer Book rubric. [9] This was an age when there had been abuses among some Evangelicals. It was not unknown for some to "go through the motions" of Baptism if, by error, no water had

---

[1] Carus, p. 600. [2] Brown, p. 68.
[3] Smyth, *Simeon and Church Order*, 1940, pp. 202–4.
[4] Published under the title of *Simeon and Church Order*, 1940.
[5] Ibid., pp. 270–81. [6] Ibid., p. 311. [7] Brown, p. 11.
[8] Brown, pp. 11–12. [9] Ibid., p. 12.

been placed in the font or for the consecrated wine at Holy Communion to be poured back into the flagons instead of being consumed by the celebrant.[1] But "Simeon's ideas were far more catholic than is usually taken for granted". He approved of fasting ("too much thought of among Papists, too little among us"); he recognized the ministry of absolution and was convinced that the benediction was more than a prayer.[2] His life was greatly influenced by his passionate love of the English Prayer Book. In his own day, some of these opinions were considered "legal" and "high-church". "What right have you", he was asked, "to care about church rule when you are holding evangelical doctrine? Shake off your churchmanship and be content to be a Christian."[3] But in Bishop Moule's words: "It was Simeon, more than even the greatest of his predecessors, who taught and exemplified the fact that the warmest Evangelical, without any real sacrifice of inter-denominational fraternity in Christ, can and should be watchfully loyal to the order and organization of the English Church in the normal exercise of his energies."[4] It was surely Simeon's intense love for the Church of England that influenced so much of his life and ministry.

No sphere appealed to Simeon for the exercise of his ministry so much as the Established Church and it is natural that he should have acknowledged this debt by being at times (as others have been) too ardent a champion of "establishment". It was on the rather curious grounds of "establishment" that he made his defence of his unusual behaviour in Scotland. "Presbyterianism is as much the established religion in North Britain as episcopacy in the South . . . as an episcopalian I preach in episcopal chapels, as a member of the established church I preach in presbyterian churches."[5] A good deal of his support of the Established Church in England came from his love of the Book of Common Prayer . . . "but the people's prejudices are in general in favour of the Establishment and the more any persons have considered the excellence of the liturgy, the more they are attached to the established church".[6] Some attacks upon it seemed to him puerile . . . "some indeed would entertain prejudices against it

[1] Ibid., pp. 80-1.   [2] Ibid., p. ix; pp. 64-5.   [3] Ibid., p. 60.
[4] H. C. G. Moule, *The Evangelical School in the Church of England; its men and its work in the nineteenth century*, 1901, quoted by Smyth, p. xv.
[5] Brown, p. 21.
[6] Sermon 194—"Excellency of the Liturgy" (sermon 4).

even if all the twelve apostles were members of it and ministered in it".[1] Simeon saw that men of his generation made the mistake common to men of all generations, . . . namely, of condemning something merely because it is open to abuse. "In general", he wrote of the Establishment, "it is want of zeal in its ministers and want of purity in its institutions that gives such an advantage to dissenters."[2] The same was true of the English liturgy: "Methinks there is scarcely a man in the kingdom that would not fall down on his knees and bless God for the liturgy of the Established Church . . . all that is wanting is an heart suited to the liturgy."[3]

But so far we have glanced only at Simeon's views on the *Established* Church and at what Canon Abner Brown calls "Simeon's sound churchmanship".[4] We shall now ask the question—what convictions lay beneath this outlook about the nature of the church itself? What doctrine of the Church did Simeon hold—what effect did it have upon his pastoral ministry and (a more difficult, though equally important question) how was his doctrine of the Church influenced by his pastoral ministry? In his sermons there are many references to the Church and—as we should expect—they are thoroughly biblical. He is anxious to define closely the Church's relationship with Our Lord. "Christ is", he declares, "the Head and Husband of the church."[5] From Revelation, he claims that the Church is "expressly represented as the wife of the Lamb" and regards Our Lord as constantly sustaining and disciplining his church . . . "and thus does our great high-priest inspect His church and people: supplying their every want and administering to them such correction as their necessities require".[6] And because he is the Head, Christ gives life to the Church. "Christ in His present exalted state is the living, the life-giving Head of His church, His church militant and His church triumphant."[7] Jesus was the "Founder of the Church" (here Simeon's theology has a twentieth-century ring) who came "riding triumphant into Jerusalem".[8] Simeon describes the excellency of the Church with many flowery descriptions of her loveliness and beauty and speaks of her most glorious

[1] Ibid.　　　　　[2] Ibid.
[3] Sermon 193—"Excellency of the Liturgy" (sermon 3).　　[4] Brown, p. 11.
[5] Sermon 2040—"Godly Jealousy the duty of ministers."
[6] Sermon 2481—"Epistle to Ephesus."
[7] Sermon 2096—"Christ the Head of the Church."
[8] Sermon preached before the University of Cambridge, 18 February 1821.

union with him, "Christ as a Bridegroom, the Church as His spouse".[1]

There are also in the sermons many corporate terms applied to the Church. She is "the fold of Christ",[2] "Christ's mystical body",[3] and Simeon uses that term which makes a special appeal to most of us . . . "the Church is one great family".[4] But how is this theme worked out? What is our status in this mystical body and our relationship one with another? Certainly we are invited to share in the same relationship with Christ as the "Church" already enjoys—"Christ as a Bridegroom and the Church as His spouse . . . into this relationship Christ is desirous to bring us all. We come in His name, to invite you to unite yourselves with Him".[5] And again, he dwells on our great calling as members of the Church— "that sinners so guilty, so polluted as we are, should be admitted into so near and so endearing a relation with the Incarnate God; how wonderful! How surpassing all knowledge and all conception. Yet it is so; and both the Church at large and every member of it is a partaker of this honour".[6] Here we are brought face to face with an apparent paradox in Simeon's thought. If we share the relationship which the "Church" already enjoys, what is this "Church" apart from its members? And again, what does this distinction between "the Church at large" and "every member of it" mean? The answer is that Simeon (in the current theological fashion) often thinks of the Church as a religious idea rather than as a corporate body. There can be little doubt that he is influenced—at any rate sub-consciously—by the distinction in Reformation theology between a visible and invisible Church. Here the organized visible Church (where the Gospel is preached and the sacraments administered) is conceived of as God's instrument for the promotion of the true invisible Church.[7]

There are—broadly speaking—two weaknesses which are closely interwoven in Simeon's doctrine of the Church as seen at any rate in most of his sermons. The first is that he comes near to

[1] Sermon 849—"The Church's Fellowship with Christ."
[2] Sermon 2194—"The Ministerial Character Portrayed."
[3] Sermon 1001—"Excellency of the Church of Christ."
[4] Sermon 2350—"The Duty of People and the Responsibility of Ministers."
[5] Sermon 849—"The Church's Fellowship with Christ."
[6] Sermon 2040—"Godly Jealousy the duty of ministers."
[7] See Leonard Hodgson, *The Doctrine of the Church as Held and Taught in the Church of England*, 1946, p. 17.

thinking of the Church as little more than the gathering together of individual believers. The Church is described as "those who flock to Christ as doves to their windows".[1] And while he admits that "every believer is a member of Christ", he goes on to say that "the whole collective number form his entire body".[2] Human beings are "constituent parts of God's spiritual temple".[3] The second weakness—closely allied to the first—is that, because the members are thought of as a "collective number", their duties are thought of individually rather than corporately. Thus, from our membership in the body, we learn: (1) our duty towards him, (2) our security in him, (3) our happiness through him.[4] Again, Simeon lists the four duties of members of the Church as follows: to submit to him, to trust in him, to rejoice in him, and to walk in his steps.[5] These are vital Christian duties, but they cannot surely be the sum-total of our duties as members of Christ's Body when they make no reference to our relationship with other members of the Body. But because—as we shall try to see more fully later—Simeon's pastoralia was in advance of his theology (a characteristic, perhaps, of Evangelical practice),[6] he describes the true spirit of the Church which most certainly does involve our relationship with each other. "We should not suffer little circumstances to alienate us from each other . . . but it is necessary that we cultivate charity and maintain the unity of the Spirit in the bond of peace."[7]

It should, I think, be observed in passing that this concentration on the individual rather than the corporate side of our religion is not—as is sometimes thought—peculiar to the Evangelicals. "If the Oxford Movement had done nothing else besides restoring this crucial idea of the Church", wrote Dr N. P. Williams, "it would still have laid English-speaking Christendom under a profound obligation."[8] However true or untrue this generalization may be, it is indisputable that the Tractarians—along with an exaltation of the Catholic Church—did not ignore the individual

---

[1] Sermon 731—"The Gospel a Source of Happiness."
[2] Sermon 2096—"Christ the Head of the Church."
[3] Sermon 1001—"Excellency of the Church of Christ."
[4] Sermon 2096—"Christ the Head of the Church."
[5] Sermon 1921—"Universality of Christ's Kingdom."
[6] See Canon Theodore O. Wedel, The Coming Great Church, 1947, pp. 24-5.
[7] Sermon 1921—"Universality of Christ's Kingdom."
[8] N. P. Williams, Northern Catholicism, 1933, p. 198.

side of the Christian Faith. Newman, as an Anglican, recognized "two only supreme and luminously self-evident beings, the soul and its Maker".[1] And Dean Church, in one of his sermons, said that "Christianity addresses itself primarily and directly to individuals. In its proper action, its purpose and its business is to make men saints; what it has to do with souls is far other, both in its discipline and its scope, from what it has to do with nations and societies".[2]

What we might describe as a "static" doctrine of the Church was common to both wings of the Church of England. But, as far as Simeon was concerned, it was never solely a static doctrine. As we have already seen, a plea for the "unity of the Spirit and the bond of peace" came bursting through and what parish priest is there who would not account this of the very essence of the Christian ecclesia? Also bursting through came that which can never be contained in any static theology of the Church— Simeon's missionary zeal. The members of the Church may only be thought of as "the whole collective number", but—says Simeon—"our anxiety should extend to the Jewish Church and to the whole world: we should desire not only to prosper in our own souls but to see Jerusalem, even the church of the living God, prospering also, so as to be a praise in the earth".[3] In Simeon's theology, members of the Church may centre their thoughts on individual salvation ("we are all concerned in the first place to seek salvation for ourselves");[4] yet he tells us that we must not only seek to become members of the Church—"let us endeavour to promote the establishment of it in all the world".[5]

But this is not the complete picture. In the index at the end of the twenty-first volume of the *Horae Homileticae*, a sermon entitled "Christians One in Heart" is not listed among the numerous references to the "Church". This is a curious (and perhaps significant) fact—evidence of a gulf between the "Church" as Simeon described it and the "Church" as he discovered it to be. For the thoughts expressed in this sermon have undoubtedly been conveyed to him from practical pastoral experience. The sermon

[1] J. H. Newman, *Parochial and Plain Sermons*, Vol. I, p. 23.
[2] R. W. Church, *The Discipline of the Christian Character*, p. 338. I am indebted for the references to Newman and Church to Dr Elliott-Binns, *English Thought 1860–1900, The Theological Aspect*, 1956, p. 263.
[3] Sermon 1010—"Duty of Interceding for the Church."
[4] Ibid.   [5] Sermon 1001—"Excellency of the Church of Christ."

begins by a recognition of the fact that, to the outside world, the Church has not been the Church—"it has been said to the reproach of Christianity that the professors of it have no union among themselves either of sentiment or affection".[1] This had been John Wesley's discovery too—"look east, west, north, or south, name what parish you please, is Christian fellowship there?"[2] Though Simeon's reaction to this situation was profoundly different from Wesley's, both recognized the absence of the living Church in English parochial life. Simeon knew that the Christian faith involves the Christian Church, sharing a common *koinonia* through the ministry of the Word and the Sacraments—"but where vital piety exists, there is found a union which obtains in no other society under heaven. . . . Christianity brings men not only into one body but into a oneness of heart and affection".[3] A later age might wish for a small but vital alteration in the wording of this sentence so that it might read: "Christianity *because* it brings men into one body (i.e. the Body of Christ) brings them into a oneness of heart and affection."

But it is surely remarkable that Simeon—in an age of great religious individualism—perceived the necessity not only of a corporate life but that this life must have an external and visible side. It is—"by baptism we are brought into one body . . . he is no sooner baptized into the faith of Christ than he becomes a member of Christ's mystical body".[4] This Body may contain differences—"on some points of doctrine, some embracing one mode of church government and some another, but united in the leading points of repentance towards God and faith in Our Lord Jesus Christ".[5] This entry into the Body is effected by baptism but "the ordinance of confirmation as administered in the Established Church is of the utmost importance"[6] . . . "I always lead the young to regard it as a preparatory step to communion rather than as an object in itself".[7] And speaking of Holy Communion: "Those who are at liberty should attend as often as they can . . . to come to the Lord's Table as some do at the three festivals of the

---

[1] Sermon 1983.

[2] Letter to the Rev. Vincent Perronet, 1748 (*Letters of John Wesley*, Standard Ed., 1931, II, p. 295).

[3] Sermon 1983—"Christians One in Heart."

[4] Sermon 1983—"Christians One in Heart." [5] Ibid.

[6] Sermon 1761—"The Ethiopian Eunuch's Confession."

[7] Sermon 193—"The Excellence of the Liturgy."

church and neglect it all the year beside is to show at once that they enter not into the true spirit of that ordinance."[1]

Although we get the impression from a good many of the sermons that Simeon is tied to a "static" doctrine of the Church which is partly influenced by Reformation theology, reluctant to apply the New Testament language to the visible Church, the truth is continually brought home to him that the visible Church can and does experience the kind of life outlined in the New Testament. This realization springs directly from Simeon's everyday experiences as a parish priest. Simeon knew that the whole life of the Church was to suffer when he was prevented by his churchwardens (on the dubious argument that he was merely a curate-in-charge) from delivering an evening lecture at Trinity Church.[2] He therefore hired a room for the purpose of holding it and as he had not a sufficiently large one in his own parish, hired one just outside. Careful as Simeon was to avoid irregularities of the kind of which other Evangelical churchmen were guilty and he himself had sometimes committed in his youth ("O spare me, spare me, I was a young man then",[3] he exclaimed when reminded of them in his old-age), this strange feature of his ministry continued for many years and was justified on the ground that it prevented a drift to nonconformity. But there seems to have been more to these meetings than this for we are given a hint that, without them, the life of the Church could not be experienced. "Where nothing is established", he says, "the members of the church are only as a rope of sand and may easily be scattered with every wind of doctrine or drawn aside by any proselytising sectary . . . what influence can a minister maintain over his people if he does not foster them as a brood under his wings?"[4] And though Simeon faced the hostility of many members of his congregation at Trinity Church, and (not unnaturally), incurred the disapproval of his bishop, his own judgement was that without these meetings "a people will never be kept together; nor will they ever feel related to their minister as children to a parent; nor will the minister himself take that lively interest in their welfare which is both his duty and his happiness".[5] It

[1] Sermon 1761—"The Ethiopian Eunuch's Confession."
[2] Service on Sunday mornings was at an hour when only the more well-to-do could attend. See Smyth, *Simeon and Church Order*, 1940, pp. 284–5.
[3] Carus, p. 278.   [4] Ibid., pp. 138–9.   [5] Carus, p. 339.

may also be argued that the conversation parties formed a similar (though much less important and uncontroversial) part of his ministry. All this surely finds a modern parallel in the often-heard cry of the parish-priest that the Church cannot exist through Sunday worship alone but through its whole life, and though this may not necessarily be achieved by sponsoring an ever-increasing number of "church-organizations", there must in addition to Sunday worship be fellowship within the body, service given by members of the body and meeting together for prayer, study, and discussion, or just for a cup of tea and a bun in the church hall. In Simeon's case, the means by which he felt forced to establish the Church's life involved a serious breach of ecclesiastical etiquette and the step was not taken lightly. "I therefore committed the matter to God in earnest prayer and entreated of him."[1] Venn was asked by Simeon's friends to reason with him, but when Simeon had explained his predicament, Venn's advice was—"Go on, and God be with you."[2] Smyth has described how Simeon consulted John Wesley too, and rode over to see him.[3] It was, of course, through the "religious societies" that Wesley had experienced the common life of the Church: "I spent Wednesday and Thursday with much satisfaction with a very loving and lively people increasing in grace as well as in number and adorning the doctrine of God our Saviour . . . they are of one heart and of one mind striving for the hope of the Gospel."[4] And Charles Wesley writes in his hymns of the corporate life they had experienced:

> Christ from whom all blessings flow,
> Perfecting the saints below
> Hear us, who Thy nature share
> Who Thy mystic body are.[5]

Most of this experience of the "common life of the church" had been gained outside the Established Church, without the Established Church's blessing. But who can reasonably doubt that those who enjoyed this experience discovered a vital element of the New Testament Church which was so sadly lacking in the life of the Establishment? Indeed, far from being—as is sometimes

[1] Ibid., pp. 45–6.   [2] Ibid., p. 46.
[3] Smyth, *Simeon and Church Order*, 1940, pp. 286–7.
[4] *The Journal of John Wesley*, Standard Ed., 1938, VII, pp. 213–14.
[5] See No. 720 in *The Methodist Hymn Book* (1933 ed.). The hymn is entitled "The Church".

supposed—purely individualistic in their approach, the eighteenth-century Evangelicals had a real experience of the Church's corporate life, and this corporate experience was—as the present Principal of Wycliffe Hall has said—"the most distinctive thing about them".[1]

But—at any rate as far as the Church of England is concerned—it is a matter for profound thankfulness that Charles Simeon was able to experience and promote the "common life of the church" within the bounds of the Established Church. As we have seen, owing to the peculiar and unfortunate difficulty of not being permitted to gather the whole Christian family within the walls of his parish church or even within the bounds of his parish, Simeon decided after much heart-searching to break one of the rules of the Establishment in an attempt to bring Christians of one heart into one body. But though it is true that these meetings continued after Simeon was able to hold his Sunday-evening lecture at Trinity Church, and though the whole project ended in chaos and much bitterness, he regarded it as vital to express the full life of the Church, even if it could only be an interim measure.[2] All this is not meant to justify the holding of meetings in someone else's parish, but it is meant to explain it and to show how Simeon reached a conviction that only thus could he minister to his flock as one body in Christ. But in the remaining years of his ministry this Christian *koinonia* developed on a more regular pattern. For Simeon encouraged participation by the laity not only in church administration but in the pastoral life of the parish: "The minister is the pastor . . . he has more to do in the closet and study than even in the cottage. Let him nominate elders, laymen, and laywomen to visit the sick, to pray with them and to read to his people. I do not wholly approve of prayer meetings nor would have these elders help in this way but in visiting the people."[3] Here was truly the Church at work.

Simeon's concept of the Church—experienced fully but only partially defined—lived and grew and had its being within the Church of England and did not need an "unfettered" existence outside. After Simeon, the Evangelicals became far more individualistic in their pursuit of a negative anti-Roman polemic. Had

---

[1] F. J. Taylor on "The Church and the Ministry" in *Evangelicals Affirm in the Year of the Lambeth Conference*, 1948, p. 132.
[2] Carus, pp. 339-41.   [3] Brown, pp. 217-18.

Simeon been alive later in the century, he would "without wish or effort on his part become the leader of a very large middle party".[1] In making this emphasis on the individual, the Evangelicals tended to fall back upon that conception of the "invisible church" which has always haunted post-Reformation Protestant theology. The visible Church was regarded merely as a "scaffolding by means of which the spiritual building could best advance".[2] Because the visible Church is full of imperfections—tares in the wheat and bad fish in the drag-net[3]—there is a constant fear lest it should be identified with the kingdom of God. It was partly through this fear that the Evangelicals were reluctant to bring their theology into line with their experience of the Church's common life. In this century—and particularly in the last twenty years—Evangelical theology (while still alive to the "identification" danger) has shown a real concern for the Church as the Body of Christ.[4] A living experience of it—with a subsequent diminution of "party" views and "party" spirit—has carried men in heart and mind back to Apostolic days. Simeon's doctrine—for all its limitations—did reflect this same living experience which he was able to hold within the gentle but sustaining arms of the Ecclesia Anglicana.

[1] Ibid., p. 65.

[2] T. W. Drury, R. B. Girdlestone and H. C. G. Moule, *English Church Teaching*, 1914, p. 162.

[3] Leonard Hodgson, *The Doctrine of the Church as Held and Taught in the Church of England*, 1946, p. 18.

[4] F. J. Taylor, *The Church of God*, 1946, p. 96.

6

SIMEON AND THE MINISTRY

MICHAEL HENNELL

Simeon and the Ministry

URING THE fifty-four years that he was Vicar of Trinity Church, Cambridge, Charles Simeon did much to establish a tradition of ministry which had incalculable influence on the work and character of a vast body of Anglican clergy in this country and in many other parts of the world. This he did both by example and by training.

The pattern of ministry Simeon established at Trinity Church was in many ways similar to that found in many other parishes where the incumbent was Evangelical. The emphasis on the ministry of the Word and the centrality of the Cross; the reverent use of, and devotion to, the Book of Common Prayer; the revival of sacramental life; the dividing up of the faithful into classes for instruction and prayer and into bands of district visitors for administering poor relief; the use of tracts; the gathering together like-minded neighbouring clergy into a clerical society; the over-coming of initial hostility from a congregation fearful of change and "enthusiasm"; the Christian leavening of social and civic life: all this was to be found in the parishes of Robinson at Leicester, Biddulph at Bristol, and John Venn at Clapham, as well as in Simeon's parish. As in the case of John Venn, Simeon found that there was only provision for two services on Sunday: the morning service, which he took himself, and the afternoon service, which was taken by a lecturer.[1] Against much opposition both men established an evening lecture to reach the poor, Simeon's service being originally intended for college servants who could not attend at another time. It is not really surprising that the parochial pattern at Holy Trinity, Clapham, and Trinity, Cambridge, should have been so similar for both were carefully trained and advised

---

[1] The Rev. John Hammond resigned five years after Simeon's appointment as vicar. Another nominee of the opposition group succeeded him; Simeon was himself elected lecturer in 1794 and in 1808 moved the lecture, with his parishioners' consent, to the evening, leaving himself with two Sunday services.

by John Venn's father, Henry Venn, formerly Vicar of Huddersfield, whom Simeon looked up to as "a father, an instructor and a
most bright example".[1] Henry Venn was easily accessible to
Simeon; during the first twelve and critical years of his ministry
Venn was resident at Yelling Rectory. Behind all Simeon's great
influence lies that of Henry Venn. It was Henry Venn who taught
Simeon that disregard for parochial boundaries may have been a
necessary evil in the early days of the Evangelical Revival but it
had to be abandoned if the Evangelical movement was to remain
within the Church of England.[2] It was this strict loyalty to the
Church of England, its officers, its system, and its ordinances,
that Simeon practised himself and instilled into the long succession of ordinands who looked up to him for guidance and
training.[3]

I

Simeon was fully aware of the opportunity God had given him
when he gave him Trinity Church. "Trinity Church", he once
said, "holds about nine hundred, without the children and it is
filled. But many of those who hear me are legions in themselves,
because they are going forth to preach, or else to fill stations of
influence in society. In that view I look upon my position here
as the highest and most important in the kingdom, nor would I
exchange it for any other. If you have dukes and nobles to hear
you, they seldom attend to what you say. Not so the congregation
at Cambridge."[4] In term time he said that he hardly ever prepared
a sermon without the students in view, especially on Sunday
evening, when they, and not the college servants, formed the bulk
of his congregation.

However, it was not only in the pulpit of his church, but in
his rooms in college that Simeon sought to influence the future
clergy and lay leaders of the Church of England. With regard to
the former, Simeon tried to supply what was sadly lacking: a
systematic training for the ministry. During Simeon's life-time
there were no degree courses in theology.[5] Although from the
early sixteenth century there had been two divinity professors at

[1] Carus, p. 23.
[2] C. H. E. Smyth, *Simeon and Church Order*, 1940, p. 281.
[3] Ibid., *passim*.   [4] Brown, p. 176.
[5] These were not established till the late nineteenth century.

both universities there were few lectures till 1780 when the Norrisian Professorship in Revealed Religion was established at Cambridge. The Norrisian Professor was required to give fifty lectures a year. The Bishops required all Cambridge ordination candidates to present a certificate proving that they had attended a certain number of these.[1] At Oxford there was no equivalent course.

In spite of many attempts since the Reformation to provide more specialized training for the ministry, nothing more was required by the bishop nor provided by the universities;[2] the view being that a general education was sufficient as it was for all the other learned professions at that time. Simeon set out to remedy this situation as far as one individual don could. Through his sermon classes and "conversation parties", Simeon sought to supply what he himself, as an undergraduate, had looked for in vain. In 1790 Simeon started his sermon classes on Sunday evenings for ordinands. His "conversation parties", which were open to all members of the University, did not begin till 1812. Our fullest information about both groups is derived from the years 1827 to 1830 of which Abner Brown and William Carus have both left accounts. By that time both parties were held on Fridays—the "conversation party" at 6 p.m. and the sermon class at 8 p.m. The former was weekly during term, the latter every fortnight.

The problem of a preaching clergy had bothered the leaders of the Anglican Church since the Reformation. Cranmer found it better to provide homilies for most of his clergy to read than to license them to preach. Elizabeth's archbishops continued Cranmer's practice and it was one of the chief complaints of the Puritans that the majority of the clergy were "no preachers" but "dumb dogges". After the Restoration the Homilies seem to have been abandoned, but the practice of reading other men's compositions persisted. As late as 1806 a typical conscientious country clergyman was portrayed as one who "preaches regularly" and "takes the pains of writing out the best sermons he can find".[3] It was from this practice that Simeon sought to wean his students.

Simeon's own practice was to preach from notes. After the

[1] D. A. Winstanley, *Unreformed Cambridge*, 1935, p. 176.
[2] See F. W. B. Bullock, *A History of Training for the Ministry*, 1955.
[3] *Letters to a Young Clergyman*, published in *Christian Observer*, 1806, pp. 208–9. The anonymous author was John Venn of Clapham. See M. M. Hennell, *John Venn and the Clapham Sect*, 1958, p. 13.

service he would write out more fully the principal headings and subject matter, leaving them much as they are to be found in the twenty-one volumes of the *Horae Homileticae*. During his early years at Trinity Church he was prevented, as we have seen, from preaching at any but the morning service. This allowed him to preach for others later in the day. For these occasions he re-wrote old sermons giving special attention to their shape and construction, and fashioning them into a set pattern. Ten or twelve years later he read *Essay on the Composition of a Sermon* by the seventeenth-century French Reformed minister, Jean Claude. "From seeing my own views thus reduced to system, I was led to adopt the resolution of endeavouring to impart to others the little knowledge I possessed in that species of composition; and to adopt Claude as the ground-work of my private lectures; correcting what I thought wrong in him, and supplying what I thought deficient. . . . For the space of about twenty years I have persevered in having a few young men to assist in thus preparing for that which is generally esteemed so difficult—the writing of their sermons; and from the many acknowledgements which have been made by ministers from time to time, I have reason to hope that my labours have not been in vain in the Lord."[1]

The first sermon classes were held in his rooms in King's on Sunday evenings after church. Thomas Thomason, who came up to Magdalene in 1792, tells a correspondent: "Mr Simeon watches over us as a shepherd over his sheep. He takes delight in instructing us, and has us continually at his rooms. He has nothing to do with us as it respects our situation at college. His Christian love and zeal prompt him to notice us." In a letter to his mother he says more of what actually took place. "God has heaped upon me more favours than ever. Mr Simeon has invited me to his Sunday evening lectures. This I consider one of the greatest advantages I ever received. The subject of his lectures is natural and revealed religion. These he studies and puts together with much pains and attention. He reads the fruits of his labours to us, and explains it. We write after him. He then dismisses us with prayer."[2] Here was a series of lectures on a favourite theological subject in the eighteenth century, possibly chosen because it would not excite suspicion. Very soon Simeon seems to have replaced the lecture

---

[1] Carus, pp. 61–2. The passage is an extract from the memoir of his own life that Simeon wrote in 1813.　　　　　[2] Ibid., p. 97.

by the sermon class proper, using his own edition of Claude's essay as a text-book. Instruction in elocution was also given. Attached to Simeon's edition of Claude's essay were a hundred skeletons of sermons he had himself preached. These became the basis of the *Horae Homileticae*. In these Simeon was consciously trying to supplement the Homilies of which he fully approved, but which he considered omitted many essential topics. The skeletons themselves were intended to be used by young clergy as the framework from which their own sermons could be written; this is made quite plain in the Preface to the *Horae Homileticae*. In this way Simeon broke the tradition of the borrowed sermon and produced a succession of men who preached expository sermons according to an accepted pattern.

In 1828 when Abner Brown began to attend the sermon class on alternate Fridays in term, he found the class numbered between fifteen and twenty men. At the beginning of the academic year those who wished to attend had to take the initiative by calling on Simeon who gave them an invitation for the term, adding that he hoped his callers would attend regularly as each term had its own syllabus. The class lasted an hour, at the end of which Simeon gave a text to be treated in some special way and read next time. Next time each man read his sermon outline, and Simeon criticized it orally and made suggestions for improving it.[1] Added to instruction in sermon composition Simeon gave careful training in voice-production, reading, and delivery from the pulpit. Here are some of the points he made:

"1. Form your voice, not in your chest, nor in your throat, nor in the roof of your mouth, but simply with your lips and teeth. . . .

2. Deliver your Sermons, not pompously, but as a professor *ex cathedra*, and as a father to his family. To get ease, read parts of your Sermon to an ideal person (any object, as your inkstand, or candlestick), and then repeat *the same words* in a way of common oral instruction; and repeat this, till you perceive (as it were) that your ideal person clearly understands you.

3. Let there be the same kind of pause, and of emphasis as a man has in conversation when he is speaking on some important subject."[2]

[1] Brown, p. 51. [2] Carus, p. 685.

These are the words of a man who knows what he is talking about: it is not surprising that Abner Brown should claim that the advice offered at the sermon classes was "what few could easily forget".[1]

The "conversation party" was open to all members of the university, not only to ordinands, though they almost certainly composed the majority of those who attended. It was a bigger and less formal gathering than the sermon class and seems to have been in the nature of a one-man "brains trust".

The opportunity for entertaining between forty and sixty undergraduates at a time came when Simeon moved his rooms from the bottom to the top of Gibbs' Building. His new rooms were larger than those on the ground floor and were divided by two passages each of which Simeon fitted with numerous hat-pegs. He also supplied door-mats and a scraper. He filled his drawing-room with benches and when these were occupied later arrivals sat in the window recesses. Simeon greeted each student in turn, taking the names of any newcomers. In due course he would seat himself on a high mahogany stool and say, "Now,—if any of you have any question to ask,—I shall be happy to hear it,—and to give what assistance I can."[2] When the questions had started two waiters entered and handed round tea to the guests.

One would judge from the account that Carus has extracted from the *Christian Lady's Magazine* that the questions were generally concerned with Biblical exposition,[3] but Abner Brown shows that those asked at parties he attended in the late 1820s were much wider and more topical; they included Slavery, Repeal of the Test and Corporation Acts, Roman Catholic Emancipation, Parliamentary Reform, Municipal and Ecclesiastical Reform, and State aid to Education.[4]

With the questioners Simeon was extremely patient; he reserved his irritability for those who had failed to use the mats or the scraper and covered his carpets with gravel from the college paths and for others who leant nonchalantly against a suite of marble tables he had inherited.

Abner Brown says that during the three years he attended the "conversation parties" there was considerable difference of opinion as to their value. Some attended regularly throughout their three years, others complained of the sameness of the parties

[1] Brown, p. 51.   [2] Carus, p. 649.   [3] Ibid., pp. 648–54.
[4] Brown, p. 64.

and presumably attended less regularly or ceased coming altogether. Brown defends Simeon, saying that though the freshmen each year asked the same questions as their predecessors had done, Simeon seldom answered the same question in the same way and usually employed different illustrations. Second and third year men who persisted inclined to produce more varied and profound questions. Brown appreciated some repetition but found something new each Friday. However, he admitted that there were others who complained that Simeon's remarks were "trite, obvious, and commonplace".[1]

Of those who attended, none was invited. In 1823 numbers reached forty; by 1827 they were nearer sixty. Of those present many became parochial clergy, colonial chaplains, and missionaries; others became lawyers, soldiers, and members of other professions. It may be hazarded that the influence of Simeon on the officers of the Indian army was a prime cause of the extension of the work of the Church Missionary Society in India during the nineteenth century.

Most of those who attended came from two colleges, Magdalene and Queens'.[2] All who came were labelled "Sims". It seems that the term "Simeonite" was a title they themselves invoked. Those who stayed up to read during the Long Vacation were known as "the remnant of the Simeonites".[3]

On all "Sims", whether ordinands or not, Simeon imposed certain obligations. These were hard work, daily exercise, and unfailing obedience to the university statutes. "Exercise", he would say, "constant, regular, and ample, is absolutely essential to a reading man's success." He told his students to walk every day to the three mile stone out of Cambridge and see that no one had taken it away.[4] Simeon himself rode out each day "unless my work or the weather render it particularly inconvenient".[5] Even devotional study of the Bible must not be allowed to interfere with regular systematic reading for a degree. "You come here for study", Simeon told his students, "for discipline of mind, for

---

[1] Brown, p. 44.

[2] "Forty years ago I had none but Magdalene men at my parties" (Brown, p. 191). This was because of the Tutor, William Farish. To Magdalene Evangelical parents sent their sons and the Elland Society their candidates. When Isaac Milner became President of Queens' in 1788 some chose his college. Few of Simeon's followers seem to have come from his own college.

[3] Brown, p. 62.   [4] Brown, p. 126.   [5] Carus, p. 165

the acquisition of knowledge. . . . Your duty to God requires you to devote your time and energy to the University course of study; and your Bible reading must be confined to the leisure which you have after spending the proper hours in University study and necessary exercise."[1] Simeon even went as far as to say that theological study of the Bible "belongs more to the time when we have occasion to be always in the Bible—when we are in a parish. At that time studies of a general or secular nature are out of place".[2] However, at college general information as well as facts for examinations must be acquired. This narrowing down of a parson's intellectual concerns after ordination is surely one of the few weaknesses of Simeon's plan of ministerial training.

There were also other gatherings, more informal than the sermon class or the "conversation party". If there were staying in Cambridge a missionary or one of Simeon's prominent clerical or lay friends, Simeon would hold a dinner party in his rooms and invite the students in after hall. There was no set procedure, but the evening always concluded with family prayers consisting of Bible exposition and prayer. On these occasions, ladies were usually present.

Simeon was not only a pioneer in training clergy for their office, he was also probably the first man to do anything for clergy wives. He once said to them: "Ministresses, half-ministers" are "often the more important and useful half in your husbands' parishes."[3] He asked his students to find out the names of any married undergraduates they might see attending his church; he then invited husband and wife to dinner. Some of these married men would be ordinands. Further the Cambridge Clerical Society, of which Simeon was leader, was the only clerical club to which wives were invited. The conference was residential; the guests arrived one week-day evening and departed three mornings later.[4] While the men discussed "biblical and parochial subjects", their wives "compared their own schemes for local usefulness". In the

---

[1] Brown, p. 36. Simeon used to illustrate his point by suggesting that his cook or his coachman might excuse themselves from their work by saying they were reading the Bible. The cook might say, "Sir, I was busy reading the Word of Life, and could not attend to the dinner sooner." Should I not constantly reply, "Did I engage you to read the Bible during hours that were mine, or to cook my dinner when and as I want it? Your Bible will do you no good, cook, for you are stealing the time which in God's providence is mine, not yours, and using it for your own purposes."

[2] Ibid., p. 194.   [3] Brown, p. 165.   [4] Carus, p. 269.

evenings they had a session together with a suitable subject for discussion.[1]

Simeon was also concerned that men called to the ministry should not be prevented by lack of financial means from coming up to the university. Funds for Evangelical candidates were administered by the Elland and Bristol Education Aid Societies,[2] but by 1820 Simeon felt the need for a similar society in London; he therefore founded the London Clerical Aid Society which from its inauguration supported twenty men. He was also concerned with the after-care of his clergy. Many a "Sim", when revisiting Cambridge, would find money pressed into his hand for some parochial scheme.

During the last years of his life the significance of what Simeon was doing was being noted by others concerned with the same problem. In 1826 he received a visit from three bishops, Burgess of St David's, Law of Chester, and Jebb of Limerick. "I accompanied them to King's Chapel, and to Trinity Library, and spent about an hour with them."[3] Dr Bullock suggests that these three bishops during that hour discussed with Simeon his methods of training men for the ministry, for Burgess was the founder of St David's College, Lampeter, and Law of St Bees, the non-graduate theological college in Cumberland started in 1816.[4] In fact it might also be said that in rooms of King's College, Cambridge, another theological college was in existence.

We must now turn to the ideals and principles which Simeon had in view when training men for ministry in the Church of God.

II

"I most sincerely congratulate you", Charles Simeon wrote to his friend, John Venn, "not on a permission to receive £40 or £50 a year, nor on the title of Reverend, but on your accession to the most valuable, most honourable, most important, and most glorious office in the world—to that of an ambassador of the Lord

[1] Brown, p. 47 and Carus, pp. 268–70. For fuller information on Evangelical clerical societies see G. C. B. Davies, *The Early Cornish Evangelicals*, 1951, ch. IV and M. M. Hennell, *John Venn and the Clapham Sect*, 1958, pp. 83–8 and Appendix B.

[2] The Elland Society, founded in 1767, started its ordination fund ten years later. The Bristol Education Aid Society began as an ordination grants committee in 1795. [3] Carus, p. 606.

[4] F. W. B. Bullock, *A History of Training for the Ministry of the Church of England in England and Wales from 1800 to 1874*, 1955, p. 42.

Jesus Christ."[1] This high conception of the ministry Simeon consistently maintained. He held the ministerial office to be more honourable than that of kings and statesmen. "We mean not to deprecate other offices; or to place the common office of pastor on a footing with that of Prophet or Apostle; but still we must be permitted to 'magnify our office' beyond that of any earthly magistrate, as far as things visible and temporal are excelled by things invisible and eternal."[2] He believed it to be the most difficult office a man could undertake as well as the most important. "It is the most important because the salvation of multitudes depends upon it: it is the most difficult, because it requires such self-denying habits and spiritual affections. The responsibility that attaches to it is such, that no man would dare to take it upon himself, if he had not a promise of peculiar assistance in the discharge of it."[3]

A man does not take the Christian ministry on himself—he is called to it. "There is an external and there is an internal call to be a minister." Simeon explained at one "conversation party". "The external call is the ecclesiastical appointment by the Church to officiate; the internal is the entire surrender of the heart and soul to God to be for his glory and service."[4] The internal call is unlikely to come through any direct revelation, most often it comes "partly from a sense of obligation to him for his redeeming love, partly from a compassion for the ignorant and perishing multitudes around us, and partly from a desire to be an honoured instrument in the Redeemer's hands".[5] Because the call comes from God, "parents are wrong to designate young men for the ministry before they are of an age to choose that line". Because candidates require natural talents as well as supernatural grace, "even devoted men ought not to think of themselves 'called of God', unless they feel an adaptation to the work, ability to speak, or to do the duties of the office. Many mistake their calling and, with devoted hearts, are, nevertheless, out of their sphere, when they enter the ministry. They might do good in the way of parochial visitation, and yet not as preachers and stewards of God's oracles".[6]

Simeon believed that though the ministry was the most im-

[1] Carus, p. 28.   [2] Sermon 1926—"Duty of Ministers."
[3] Sermon 992—"The Ministerial Office."   [4] Brown, p. 208.
[5] Sermon 194—"Excellence of the Liturgy."   [6] Brown, p. 208.

portant of all vocations, the vocation of the Christian layman was hardly less so. In fact Simeon was opposed to men already settled in another profession deserting it for the ministry. "I am not an advocate for men leaving their lawful and settled calling, and coming into the ministry. Circumstances may indeed point it to them as their duty, but they ought to see their duty clear. We may serve God in all lawful callings; and it is better for many to serve him in a variety of lines than that all should crowd into the one, under an idea that they can serve God in no other; they ought to weigh the responsibilities of having many souls, instead of only one or two (their own family) to answer for."[1]

"Man, as a social being, has duties to the society of which he is a member: and of these duties he must be reminded, no less than of those which are purely personal. The Church of Christ is one great family, in which, as in every other family, order must be observed, by the exercise of power in those who preside, and a submission to it amongst those who are placed under their direction. The government that shall be exercised in it is appointed by God himself: who has invested his ministers with power to rule, and has required of their people a submission to their authority. But, as on the one hand, there has been amongst some who have presided an unscriptural usurpation of authority, very different from that which God ever committed to them; so on the other hand, there is amongst others a very unscriptural disregard of that authority which is legitimate, and which every minister of God is bound to exercise in that society over which he presides. For the due administration of order and good government in the Church, the Apostle, having finished his directions respecting *personal* duties, proceeds to give one, which more immediately relates to our *social* intercourse, but which is of the greatest consequence to the welfare of that family of which we are members."[2]

Although in the sermon on the Ordinal[3] the laying on of hands is only mentioned in passing, Simeon held strong convictions concerning the value of episcopal ordination. This emerges from notes taken at the "conversation party" at which the call to the ministry was being discussed. According to Simeon when "the Bishop says to the candidate 'Receive ye the Holy Ghost', he does

[1] Brown, p. 208.
[2] Sermon 2350—"The People's Duty, A Minister's Joy."
[3] Sermon 194—"Excellence of the Liturgy."

so as God's ambassador or representative, not because he (the Bishop) has it to give, but because he is the instrument by which God conveys the blessing to those who are able to receive it. In the same way the priest pronounces the benediction. He knows that to all who receive that benediction in God's appointed way of faith, it is a blessing, but not to others".[1] Simeon also held the same theory of faithful reception with regard to priestly absolution. "The Minister has no power to *forgive* sins, but he has power, if certain premisses are granted, to *absolve* sins. His power is simply declaratory and official and has no virtue in it as the Papists would have it."[2] On the other hand Simeon was also prepared to say: "In pronouncing the benediction, I do not do it as a *finale*, but I feel that I am actually dispensing peace from God, and by God's command. . . . It is not the Priest, but the priestly office, that performs Divine service. Hence, as indeed our Church declares, when the Priest happens individually to be a sinful man, he still does not defile the bread and wine which he administers in the Lord's Supper."[3]

The description in the Ordinal of priests as "messengers" and "watchmen" was entirely congenial to Simeon, but he made no clear distinction between "messengers" and "stewards of the Lord". For both the term "ambassador" was equally appropriate and it is in the sermon "Ministers, the Lord's Stewards" that he writes: "As earthly kings are represented by their ambassadors, and speak by them in foreign courts, so the Lord Jesus Christ himself speaks by his ministers: they stand in his stead; they speak in his name; their word is not their own, but his; and must be received 'not as the word of men, but, as it is in truth, the word of God'."[4] As the sermon proceeds it is quite evident that Simeon understands the term "mysteries" as relating to those of revelation.

As ambassadors Christian ministers proclaim the good news of God; as watchmen they are to warn those committed to their charge. "Ministers are described as watchmen and sentinels, placed at a distance from the camp to give warning of the enemy's approach."[5] This sentence is based on Ezekiel 33.8,[6] a verse quoted by Simeon in sermon after sermon.

[1] Brown, pp. 208–9.   [2] Ibid., pp. 209–10.   [3] Brown, p. 89.
[4] Sermon 1951.
[5] Sermon 1111—"Office and Responsibility of Ministers."
[6] "If thou dost not speak to warn the wicked from his way, that wicked man shall die in his iniquity; but his blood will I require at thine hand."

Simeon's fullest teaching on the Christian Ministry is not to be found, surprisingly enough, in his exposition of St Paul's Second Epistle to the Corinthians, but in his treatment of the second and third chapters of the First Epistle to the Thessalonians. Outstanding is a sermon entitled "The Ministerial Character Portrayed", based on 1 Thessalonians 2.7,8. Simeon expounded the same passage in greater detail to a small party in his rooms, of clergy, wives, and students. In the sermon he says that ministers are portrayed in Scripture by various figures. He mentions three: shepherd, father, and nursing mother. "St Paul, declaring his anxiety for the welfare of his converts, compares his feelings with the pangs of a woman in child-birth; and his delight in them, with that of a mother cherishing in her bosom her new-born infant."[1] In the tender and selfless affection that the mother has for her baby Simeon sees the attitude which St Paul would have ministers adopt towards their people. Simeon added at the "conversation party" that the mother is "not trying to be *thought* a good mother but with her whole heart and soul being one . . . willing not only to give such things as are prepared for her infant but drawing out her own breast to give it nourishment".[2] A nursing mother has to consider her baby in the food she herself eats, "so let a Minister have an eye to his people in all the spiritual food he takes, the books he reads, the views he allows to enter his mind; in all he does, even as a private individual, lest the tone of his thoughts should become prejudiced to his flock, his sermons less nutritive for them, or stronger than they can bear".[3] A minister's spiritual health is closely bound up with that of his people, "being blessed in his own soul, he will be a blessing to all around him. . . . He is a vessel in which the golden oil is treasured up; and from which it passes, in the golden pipes of ordinances, to every lamp. If he be destitute, their light will decay; if he be full, they will burn the brighter, and God will be the more glorified in them".[4] The need of utter identification between pastor and people has seldom been more trenchantly expressed.

In the light of these passages it is not surprising that humility and gentleness were for Simeon all-important in the character of a Christian minister. Here Simeon was able to help others from

[1] Sermon 2194—"The Ministerial Character Portrayed."
[2] Brown, p. 162.   [3] Brown, pp. 163–4.
[4] Sermon 1926—"Prayer for Ministers."

experience of a battle that was being fought out in his own personality between grace and nature. By nature Simeon was proud, imperious, sensitive, fiery-tempered; a solitary individual, eager for friendship, whom others avoided because of his conceits, eccentricities, and barbed words. As he grew older, although eccentricity and punctiliousness remained, humility and love triumphed over pride and harshness, so that during the latter part of his life there can have been few men who had more friends. Simeon never tired of repeating a sentence old John Thornton had wisely written to him for his benefit: "the three lessons which a minister has to learn, 1. Humility—2. Humility—3. Humility."[1] Simeon, at the age of sixty, looking back on his own ministry, wrote: "I would have conscious unworthiness to pervade every act and habit of my soul; and whether the woof be more or less brilliant, I would have humility to be the warp."[2] It was in humility that he found the preaching of "pious ministers defective". "I do not see", he said, "so much as I could wish, an holy reverential awe of God."[3]

With humility Simeon always linked love, the *agape* love of 1 Corinthians 13. "When reading 1 Corinthians xiii this morning I asked myself, 'How should I act towards Mr and Mrs Edwards and Mr and Mrs Thomason', and regretted that the same spirit did not animate me towards every other person. I began to pray for our Provost, and Mr Flower, and Mr Twiss, the grocer. I apprehend that the best mode of understanding the nature and extent of Christian love, is to consider what dispositions we shew towards the dearest objects of our affections, and to put every human being in their place."[4] Friends who did not show these characteristics could be certain of a rebuke from Simeon. To an incumbent, whose congregation complained that his style of preaching was "unnecessarily harsh and offensive, and who had dismissed a curate for voicing the congregation's complaints", Simeon writes: "Will you forgive me, my dear Friend, if I say, that in both these respects you have erred. It is not by coarseness

[1] Carus, p. 74.   [2] Ibid., p. 523.   [3] Ibid., p. 522.
[4] Quoted from Simeon's diary by Carus, p. 219. These two clerical couples were possibly the closest of Simeon's friends. Edward Edwards was a convert of Simeon's, who spent a long ministry at King's Lynn. Thomas Thomason was for many years Simeon's curate; subsequently he became Chaplain to the East India Company. Simeon, together with Thomason's mother, looked after the Thomasons' son. Most of Simeon's letters are to the Thomasons.

of expression, or severity of manner, that we are to *win* souls, but by 'speaking the truth *in love*', and if we are offended at such a suggestion being offered to us in a kind and affectionate way, it shews that humility and love have not a due ascendant over us. I did suppose, from your age and deep-rooted piety, you would have been able to fill with comfort to yourself and advantage to the people that situation, which is of singular delicacy and importance; but if I am rightly informed, your own mind is uncomfortable, and your ministrations, as under such circumstances might well be expected, breathe no more of the spirit of love than before the matter was mentioned to you."[1] Simeon goes on to suggest that it is the vicar, not the curate, who needs a change of situation. The letter ends by asking for forgiveness for himself for being so outspoken. To another he writes: "You must not be in bondage to the religious world any more than to the ungodly. True, you are not to keep back the fundamental doctrines of the Gospel: but there are different ways of stating them; and you should adopt that which expresses kindness and love, and not that which indicates an unfeeling harshness."[2] Even with regard to such a sacred topic as Sabbath-keeping Simeon was anxious to see love triumph over law. "In my own personal habit", he writes, "I am as strict as most: but in my judgement, as before God, I think that many religious characters—Ministers as well as others—are in error. I think that many Judaize too much, and that *they would have joined the Pharisees in condemning our Lord* on many occasions."[3]

Simeon considered that though clergy should be warm-hearted they should not be soft-headed; a well-regulated mind and a balanced judgement of both people and things he deemed essential.[4] He also urged his friends to be sensible about their health. "Don't let Satan make you overwork—and thus put you out of action for a long period."[5] To his old friend, Bishop Daniel Wilson of Calcutta, he wrote congratulating him in this respect: "It requires more deeply-rooted zeal for God to keep within our strength *for his sake*, than to exceed it. Look at all the young ministers: they run themselves out of breath in a year or two and in many instances never recover it. Is this wise?"[6] A year after

[1] Carus, pp. 461–2.　　　[2] Ibid., p. 469.　　　[3] Ibid., p. 692.
[4] Sermon 2240—"The Spirit of Vital Christianity."
[5] Brown, p. 166.　　　[6] Carus, p. 762.

this letter was written Simeon died at the age of seventy-seven; Bishop Wilson lived to be eighty. Both died in harness after years of effective ministry. Perhaps they have a word to say to the parish priest to-day who prides himself on never taking a day off and becomes an easy prey to mental break-down.

Few men in the whole history of the Church helped more men and women in their spiritual pilgrimage than Charles Simeon, but the secret of his effectiveness lay in his own closeness to God and his willingness to delegate to the laity, whether students or members of his congregation, those things that had to be done, but need not be done by himself personally. In 1829 he wrote to C. R. Sumner, Bishop of Winchester: "I have seen, my Lord, of very recent date a little pamphlet, wherein a Minister is set forth in Herbert's way as the Father, the Physician, etc. etc., of his Parish; but my judgement did not go along with it. In a very small parish these duties may be combined: but it appears to me that, *comparatively*, this is serving tables. A Pastor has other and higher duties to attend to. . . . The giving himself to the word of God and prayer, seems to me to be his peculiar duty; and the paternal part—of administering relief, etc.—should, I think, be delegated to others *under his superintendence*, as Moses delegated many of his duties to the seventy employed by him."[1] He then goes on to describe the duties of his team of thirty district visitors.

In serving a parish a faithful pastor must expect two things: initial hostility and ultimate success. Simeon's own experience at Trinity Church had taught him how fierce could be opposition to an Evangelical ministry, and again and again he warned candidates for the ministry not to expect wealth and popularity but ignominy and violent opposition. "If the 'signs of a Minister', or accompaniments of the Ministry, be like those of the Apostle's days, 'reproaches, necessities, and distresses for Christ's sake' and the only *pluralities* be 'labours, stripes, prisons, deaths', there will not be many candidates for the ministry,"[2] but offers will abound from those who expect to "mind the fleece only, instead of attending to their flocks".[3] But in Simeon's view to the faithful minister success would come. He could not accept the view that the fruits of a faithful ministry are unlikely to be seen in this world; at Trinity Church he had witnessed a revolution in congregation and

[1] Carus, pp. 637–8.   [2] Sermon 1493—"The Apostles Chosen."
[3] Sermon 1271—"The Ministerial Office."

students alike, and he expected the same to happen elsewhere. "Some indeed", he says in his sermon on the Ordinal, "would entertain prejudice against it (the established Church), even if all the twelve Apostles were members of it, and ministered in it: but in general, it is a want of zeal in its ministers, and not any want of purity in its institutions, that gives such an advantage to Dissenters. . . . Only let us be faithful to our engagements, and our churches will be crowded, our sacraments thronged, our hearers edified; good institutions will be set on foot; liberality will be exercised, the poor benefited, the ignorant enlightened, the distressed comforted; yea, and our 'wilderness will rejoice and blossom as the rose'."[1]

Simeon's ministry spanned the years 1782 to 1836. In no period was there such a change in the character and work of the clergy, never was a fresh sense of duty so swiftly rekindled. "Who would have thought that Thomas Lloyd's successor should have got his death while hunting," writes Simeon to a mutual friend. "How much better by attending the cholera in a cottage!"[2] Here are two standards of pastoral care; for the change from the one to the other, Charles Simeon, as much as any other man, was responsible.

[1] Sermon 194—"Excellence of the Liturgy." Simeon makes plain, in passing, that he does not mean to suggest "anything disrespectful of the Dissenters".

[2] Carus, p. 702.

7

THE INFLUENCE AND SIGNIFICANCE OF SIMEON'S WORK

ARTHUR POLLARD

The Influence and Significance of Simeon's Work

ANY MINISTRY over half a century must witness many changes, but few can have wrought so many as did that of Charles Simeon. The earnest young Evangelical, who in the penultimate decade of the eighteenth century had to endure so much opposition, could hardly have imagined the achievement that would eventually be his, and still less that that achievement would be so widely recognized in his latter years. The hundreds who gathered at his funeral in a last tribute of affection and esteem were also acknowledging the mighty works which, under God, Charles Simeon had been able to accomplish.[1]

I

What then was this man like, who from the time of that soul-shaking experience in 1779[2] to his death in 1836 was destined to achieve so much? That conversion must indeed have been all of grace, for there was nothing in the natural character of Simeon to make him say: "The thought rushed into my mind that Satan himself was as fit to attend [the Lord's Supper] as I."[3] Indeed, there is evidence that he had to conduct a lifelong struggle against the natural man:

"He was naturally of a haughty, impatient and impetuous temper, and these defects were sometimes exhibited in a way which was painful to the feelings of others. He was not always strictly observant of those rules of respect and courtesy which the conventional intercourse of life has prescribed and occasionally gave offence by an imperious mode of address. Being constitutionally of a very sensitive temperament, he has been known to express himself with undue severity on trifling and imaginary

[1] Cf. Bp. Wilson's remarks—Carus, pp. 837–8.
[2] See above, pp. 24–5.   [3] Carus, p. 6.

affronts; and, in the moment of excitement, would now and then redress his own grievances in a way which afterwards occasioned him pain and annoyance. He was fastidious in his attention to his person, dress and furniture, and over-punctilious in his observance of what he considered to be the address and manners of a gentleman."[1]

An instance of this "infirmity of temper" is given by Carus.[2] Simeon roughly chastised a servant, and Edwards of Lynn wrote a letter of reproof with the pseudonymous signature of the servant "John Softly" attached. Simeon immediately acknowledged the justice of the reproof in a reply signed "Chas. Proud and Irritable".

That ready response proceeded from the quality with which, more than any other, Simeon countered his own shortcomings. To quote Max Warren, "the deepest thing in Simeon was his humility".[3] The young man in 1788 valued the profound wisdom of old John Thornton's triple insistence on humility[4]; the elderly man on his sixty-third birthday recorded: "I spent this day, as I have for these forty-three last years, as a day of humiliation; having increasing need of such seasons every year I live."[5]

This self-discipline, however, was not merely repressive. Not only did it control his energies of temper and of spirit by diverting them from unworthy expression; it also directed them into channels of usefulness. The confidence that might at times become assertiveness was more often tremendous determination. Knowing whither he was bound, Simeon was intent that nothing should take him from his path. That precision which marks his eccentricities was frequently put to better use. The punctuality and promptitude he expected of others—of those, for instance, who came to the "conversation-parties"—he demanded no less of himself; and he demanded it, moreover, at four in the morning, the hour at which he used to rise for prayer and meditation. This rigorous practice formed part of that regularity and method

---

[1] *Memoirs of Charles Jerram*, ed. J. Jerram, 1855, p. 124. I am indebted to Rev. Michael Hennell for bringing this passage to my notice. Cf. his *John Venn and the Clapham Sect*, 1958, p. 89, n. 1.

[2] Carus, pp. 193-5.

[3] *Charles Simeon*, Church Book Room Press, 1949, p. 13.

[4] Carus, p. 74—quoted above, p. 152. The greatest influence in Simeon's spiritual development, however, was that of Henry Venn (see Smyth, *Simeon and Church Order*, ch. VI).   [5] Ibid., p. 572.

by which he ordered his whole life down to the minutest details. "Great was his particularity about a variety of little matters."[1] To some this might appear as just a further piece of eccentricity. The note which Carus appends to the passage is, however, illuminating: "He used to say, he thought it not beneath his notice to attend to the dotting of an *i*, or the crossing of a *t*, or the turning the tail of a *y*, if it only made his work more perfect." *There* is his supreme concern—to make his work more perfect. To that end no effort was too great, no detail too small. And from the attainment of that end he withheld nothing. His time, talents, health, and property, all were dedicated to making his work, and that meant his service for his Master, more perfect. Speaking of his achievement, Bishop Daniel Wilson wrote:

"Circumstances, over which he had little or no control, contributed no doubt to the great result—family, station in society, liberal fortune, manners, vigour of health. These we may put out of the present question [viz., the causes of the 'striking difference between the first years and the last of his Ministry']— they were simply providential gifts."[2]

But we cannot put them out of the question, for the very reason that they were providential gifts. Simeon used them as such, with a deep sense of the responsibility that was his as custodian of these talents from on high.

Unsparing of himself, Simeon was often unsparing of others, and indeed his deepest affections lay with those, like Martyn and Thomason, who were prepared to drive themselves as he did himself, even to sacrificing their lives for the sake of the Gospel. But no man of Simeon's self-awareness could fail in generosity to his weaker brethren. As testimony of this there is his behaviour during the long persecution[3] he had to endure from both town and gown. And at the end of his life he showed a like eirenical spirit. When one college instituted a Greek Testament class at the time of Simeon's evening service, he advised members of that college to attend the class in obedience to the oath they had sworn to the master and as a lesson to themselves in self-denial.[4] Simeon's natural temper cannot easily have acquiesced in such advice; when

---

[1] Ibid., p. 682.   [2] Ibid., p. 839.

[3] It is good for us to remember that this was not a matter only of the first years of Simeon's ministry. His services were disturbed as late as 1810 (Carus, p. 93).

[4] Brown, pp. 45–6.

we remember that, his peaceable attitude is all the more to be applauded. And thus it must have struck many of those around him. No wonder dons came to admire, and undergraduates to revere, him. His own self-control enabled him to exhibit qualities and capacities which made him a resolute leader, a first-rate organizer, and a supreme inspirer of men. Simeon's triumph, by the power of God, over his own natural inclinations was the first of those many victories which were eventually to stretch from his rooms in King's to the farthest corners of the earth.

His life was one long history of unceasing endeavour—in his parish, in the University of Cambridge, through the length and breadth of Britain, and out to the Jews dispersed across Europe, to Africa, India, and China, even to the ends of the earth. Two things, closely related, directed the whole of this great effort—the glory of God and the love of souls. For these he both strove himself and taught others to strive.

II

The assessment of Simeon's influence must begin with his own parish-work. It is significant that during the whole of his ministry he was a parish clergyman—for two reasons, first, because thereby is symbolized his attachment to the Church of England and the importance he placed in that attachment, and secondly, because thereby he was able to provide an example of practical pastoralia to his undergraduate followers and out of his own experience meet the questions and problems they brought forward.

Any picture of Simeon which fails to give due emphasis to his essential Anglicanism will inevitably be distorted. Simeon's views "were what bear the name of Evangelical"; in this he was at one with Christians in many denominations. But he was, above all, "a faithful and devoted son of the Church of England".[1] The Church of England, Protestant and Reformed, was for Simeon ordained by God to be his worshipping community in this land. In other countries there might be other ways—hence his communion with the Church of Scotland when he was in that country.[2] But in England all others fell away from that ideal of Church Order to be found in the Establishment. "There is in Dissent a

[1] Brown, p. 11.
[2] Carus, ch. VI. See above, Michael Webster, "Simeon's Doctrine of the Church", p. 126.

spirit of disunion," he declared.[1] And again, "Dissent is an Evil."[2] He continued, however: "But where the Gospel truth is not declared in the Church pulpit, I dare not blame a man for going where he thinks or feels that his soul can be fed."[3] Because of the evangelical poverty and the authoritarian restraints of the Church, others had loosened their connections and even denied their allegiance. "The spirit of disunion" had manifested itself in Wesley, Berridge, Lady Huntingdon, and Haweis, to name no others. Independence might well be accompanied or followed by lop-sided doctrinal emphases and even heretical tenets. The proliferation of sects, of "enthusiasm" rampant, was (and is) the consequence of that claim to private infallibility which rejected the order of the Church.

Two aspects of Simeon's approach to the problem are important—his own treatment of Dissenters and his care to prevent the lapse of his own congregation into Dissent. Towards professed Dissenters he showed that sense of comprehensive responsibility, by which the Anglican priest regards all within his parish as within his pastoral care. At one of his "conversation-parties" he said:

"Dissenters I never know; all who live in my parish I reckon of my parish. I won't discountenance them, for I know they have a right to go where they think they can get most good, as well as I have. But I won't countenance them, because I am of the Established Church, and ought to uphold it, convinced as I am of its excellency and sufficiency."[4]

His protection of his own people can be illustrated from his early years at Trinity Church. The difficulties of those years did not end with the hostility of churchwardens and pewholders. Simeon feared the possible consequences: "What was to be done? If those whose minds were impressed by my preaching had not some opportunity of further instruction, they would infallibly go to the dissenting meetings and thus be gradually drawn away from the church."[5] He took first a small room in his own parish, and then a larger one in an adjoining parish. The necessity for this latter step he regretted, for it was a breach of Church Order.[6]

[1] Brown, p. 222.   [2] Ibid., p. 223.   [3] Ibid., p. 224.
[4] Ibid., p. 108.   [5] Carus, p. 45.
[6] This was one of the lessons which Simeon learnt from Henry Venn. For a fuller treatment of the whole of this episode, see above, Michael Webster, 'Simeon's Doctrine of the Church", p. 132.

Simeon was no itinerant, and deplored anything that might make him appear one. Apart from other reasons, he believed that: "A preacher has enough to do in his own parish; if it be too small, let him seek a larger; but let him always exert himself in his own parish."[1]

Simeon gave a loving obedience to his Church. There is something touchingly symbolic of this in that last visit to Ely which he made to pay his respect to his new diocesan, a visit as a result of which he was stricken with the illness that brought him to his death-bed. Such it may be said was the measure of Charles Simeon's love for the Church of England. For that love he was prepared to suffer much. In nothing is this better illustrated than in the spirit of meekness and concilation with which he met Bishop Dampier's ungracious attitude towards him.[2] That same spirit is found again in a letter counselling obedience to episcopal authority[3] and in the advice he gave to William Carus Wilson.[4] Wilson had been refused ordination by Bishop Law of Chester on the grounds of his Calvinism. Simeon was very distressed and felt that "the Bishop had acted a most unjustifiable part". Nevertheless, he conceded: "I believe he meant to do right."[5] Here again we see Simeon's concern for the Church and respect for her leaders. This incident reminds us also of the healing influence he exercised in the Arminian-Calvinist controversy, an influence greater, Bishop Handley Moule claims, than that of any other man.[6] The fragmentation from the Body of the Church which was so marked a feature of early Evangelicalism was stopped by Simeon, and from his time onwards Evangelicals have formed an important and respected group within the Church.

I have given this topic so much prominence, because Simeon's love for the Church cannot be overestimated. "Convinced of her excellency and sufficiency"—that was how he thought of her. On the one hand, therefore, he deplored Dissent and, on the other, opposed Roman Catholic Emancipation. Brown's testimony is here especially valuable, for he was up at Cambridge between 1827 and 1830 during the Emancipation crisis. Simeon was quite

---

[1] Brown, p. 107.   [2] Carus, pp. 273ff.   [3] Ibid., p. 383.

[4] Ibid., pp. 418-20. Wilson founded Cowan Bridge School for the daughters of clergymen. He is unsympathetically—and inaccurately—portrayed by Charlotte Brontë as Mr Brocklehurst in *Jane Eyre*.

[5] Ibid., pp. 417-18.

[6] H. C. G. Moule, *The Evangelical School in the Church of England*, 1901, p. 12.

uncompromising: "All attempts to reform the Roman Catholic Church will be vain: there must be an extermination of it as a Church, and any conversion must be of the individual."[1] He foresaw the progress of Romanism after Emancipation, and feared its accession to power: "I do not think Popery changed: if Papists get the power, they will burn us everywhere. They are bound to use every endeavour to convert or destroy Protestants."[2] Nevertheless, he saw in Emancipation an opportunity: "The Clergy should preach the great fundamental truths of religion. . . . Do not preach against purgatory, or transubstantiation, or such *branches*: go to the *root* at once. Romanists offer no salvation through Christ's one offering, but salvation through various other channels. That is the fundamental difference."[3] In these warnings we may detect something of Simeon's statesmanship. He recognized the threat and advised positive means of countering it.

Simeon was effective, because he was so positive. In nothing is this better illustrated than in his training of ordinands. It was not the intercourse of a year or two that mattered, but the influence that came from it and lasted a lifetime. Fifty generations of undergraduates sat at his feet, and then went out to minister in parishes up and down the country for long years after Simeon was dead. Even into this century there remained men who could speak of the vivid impression he had made on their lives. And the impression he made was doubtless transmitted to thousands. The Cambridge to which Simeon came in 1779 was not a particularly inspiring place. Frend's Unitarianism and Watson's Liberalism were not calculated to attract many followers; the general tone of religion was low; and such Evangelicals as there were were none of them fitted to take the lead that was so much needed. Canon Smyth has aptly summarized Simeon's mission in the words: "As Vicar of Holy Trinity, it was his object to supply to undergraduates what he himself, in his own undergraduate days, had sought in vain."[4]

Simeon, with his keen practical sense, did not begin with just any undergraduates who might be available and willing to be

---

[1] Brown, p. 289.   [2] Ibid., pp. 290–1.
[3] Ibid., p. 290. On this topic, cf. also Carus, pp. 576, 630ff.
[4] *Simeon and Church Order*, 1940, p. 140. The preceding remarks are based on Canon Smyth's excellent and extensive account.

taught. He sought to ensure that those who might profit from a University education to serve God in the ministry should not be debarred from receiving such an education. Coulthurst wrote about "the two young men whom you have so generously received into your tuition".[1] Coulthurst, a former Fellow of Sidney Sussex, was Vicar of Halifax, and his letter reminds us of Simeon's connection with the Elland Clerical Society. Over a long period of years he gave more than £3,700 to the Society for its work in preparing young men for the University and making grants to them while they were there. In addition, he acted as supervisor of the Society's grantees at Cambridge. Extending this assistance to ordinands, he announced in 1814, on the inability of the Elland and Bristol Societies to supply the need, his intention of establishing a society in London "For the education of young men at the University". As always, foremost in his thoughts is the glory of God: "I hope this will be the means of procuring many labourers for the Lord's vineyard."[2] Beyond all this there were also Simeon's manifold private benefactions, far greater than we shall ever know or, perhaps, can even imagine. One such example is to be found in his treatment of the unfortunate young poet, and an Elland grantee, Henry Kirke White.[3]

When they came within his care at University, the undergraduates learnt in the sermon-classes and "conversation-parties" the elements of doctrine, pastoralia, and homiletics.[4] With doctrine I am not here concerned, but no examination of Simeon's influence can omit some mention of the other two. We have already seen that as pastor he regarded all within his parish as within his care. That is why he was so jealous in his protection of those who sought to hear him; that also is why he was so amazingly forbearing to those who opposed him. That is why he was so energetic in practical endeavours. Whether it was services for college servants, relief in a bread-famine, provision of work, sick-visiting schemes,[5] each formed part of that sanctification of the whole of life in fulfilling the purposes of God. And if that was its meaning Godwards, manwards it was providing the pattern for that widespread local endeavour which was perhaps in the

---

[1] Carus, p. 151.   [2] Ibid., p. 404.   [3] Ibid., pp. 202–3.
[4] For a fuller treatment of Simeon's training methods see above, Michael Hennell, "Simeon and the Ministry", pp. 141–4.
[5] Carus, pp. 80–2, 173; Brown, p. 217.

aggregate no less a part of the impact that the Evangelicals made upon the social life of the nineteenth century than other more spectacular enterprises. Of these latter, the anti-slavery campaign was the greatest. On issues such as this also, the influence of Simeon may have been greater than we know, for was he not the respected friend and counsellor of the Clapham Sect?

The young men who heard and saw Simeon went out into the towns and villages of England as parochial clergy to establish schools and to forward other local enterprises. Indeed, some began before they left Cambridge. A sermon of Simeon's at Trinity Church in 1827 inspired some undergraduates to gather together a group of children from Barnwell and thus to found the Jesus Lane Sunday School.[1] "Simeonites", as his followers were called and as Evangelical undergraduates were nicknamed long after Simeon's death, no doubt also established societies in their parishes similar to those which Simeon had in his. These were based on the Methodist pattern, but with the important difference that there was no lay ministry (except during Simeon's illness and then with sad results).[2] By this method he was able to minister intimately to small groups and to enquire diligently into the spiritual condition of individuals. It was pastoral care of this kind which developed that rich spirituality that characterized Evangelical piety at its best.

Homiletics for Simeon was no less, probably more, important than pastoralia. Preaching as proclamation of the Gospel is always foremost in Evangelical emphasis. I would claim much for Simeon's achievement here, but I am glad to be able to quote an opinion far more authoritative than my own, that of Canon Smyth, who writes: "It would be difficult to exaggerate his personal influence on the development of Anglican homiletics."[3] That influence was exerted, as Canon Smyth goes on to say, through the individual Evangelical clergymen who at Cambridge had learnt from Simeon's example and precept.

The object of Simeon's preaching was three-fold—"to humble the sinner, to exalt the Saviour, and to promote holiness".[4] This was the message he wished his followers to find and to convey.

---

[1] J. C. Pollock, *A Cambridge Movement*, 1953, p. 9.
[2] Carus, pp. 138–42.
[3] *The Art of Preaching*, 1940, p. 175.
[4] Preface to *Horae Homileticae*, p. xxi.

To use his own words, he sought

> "1. To impart to young Ministers a clear view of the Gospel.
> 2. To help them to an inward experience of it in their own souls."[1]

But Simeon's was no merely soteriological message of the kind which he himself calls "ultra-Evangelical".[2] As the essays in this volume show, it was comprehensive, covering the whole Gospel. In nothing is this more evident than in that mark of his Scriptural fidelity, his insistence upon giving "to any text its just meaning, its natural bearing, and its legitimate use".[3] "Regard nothing but the mind of God in it."[4]

Then there must be scrupulous care in construction—"UNITY in the design, PERSPICUITY in the arrangement, and SIMPLICITY in the diction".[5] On sermon-construction Canon Brown has preserved for us a veritable jewel of Simeon's counsel:

"Let your sermon come naturally out of your text, 'totus, teres, atque rotundus', like the kernel out of a hazel nut; and not piecemeal, and, after much trouble to your hearers, like the kernel out of a walnut. . . . A sermon should be like a telescope: each successive division of it should be as an additional lens to bring the subject of your text nearer, and make it more distinct."[6]

A sermon was a work of art, to be moulded to perfection. It had to be a finished whole. An instructive example is provided by the "last lesson for good proficients" of the sermon-class.[7] Everything must be included; there must be nothing wanting, nor anything superfluous; and the whole must be arranged in due order. Comprehensiveness must not, however, involve complexity. Time and again Simeon interpolated in his edition of Claude's essay outlines of texts simpler than those which Claude himself had given.

He stressed order and simplicity, because he always recognized the imperative need to "consider your hearers".[8] Hence sophisticated theory and elaborate statement were to be eschewed, not only as contrary to the spirit of the Gospel, but also as inadequate as means of communication. "Many wonder that . . . I do not seek

---

[1] Carus, p. 717.   [2] Preface to *Horae Homileticae*, p. xxv.
[3] Ibid., p. xxvii.   [4] *Horae Homileticae*, XXI, p. 307.
[5] Ibid., p. vi.   [6] Brown, p. 183.   [7] Carus, pp. 643–5.
[8] Ibid., pp. 186, 726; Brown, pp. 182–3.

out new and remarkable views. But such a practice I abhor. It is not primarily God's truth, but self. . . . I want to get the marrow out of every passage, and make a valuable commentary for the use of the Church."[1] We also see here another reason for simplicity; there must be no opportunity for self-glory to obscure God's glory.

But if Simeon respected the intellect of his audience, he respected also their feeling. The sermon must be "affecting"; yet the result must be not mere animal spirits, but a true godly affection. Demonstrativeness in the "way of enthusiasm"[2] he suspected. Speaking of a special Week in 1816—possibly Bible Week[3]—he stated: "I look forward to it with joy; though, in fact, it borders too much upon religious dissipation";[4] and in a wonderful tribute to Thomason he made a forceful contrast:

"His religion was of a marvellous kind; it consisted in brokenness[5] of spirit and lowliness before God, and humility before men. I care not for religion which is not of this kind; but it is rare. Young men come up to college, all activity and zeal, but they are in general not humble. . . . The religion of 'the religious world' is spurious,—wants humility, which is at the base of all real religion; it is all Committees, Societies, and so forth, but where is the humility, the esteeming others better in honour, the willing to be the worst of all, the servant of all? Yet that was Thomason."[6]

Simeon's counsel against undue emotion does not, however, mean that he avoided emotion. His own temperament was too warm for that to be possible. Brown asks: "Whoever heard a dry sermon from Simeon's lips?";[7] and Carus testifies: "The intense fervour of his feelings he cared not to restrain; his whole soul was in his subject, and he spoke and acted exactly as he felt."[8] Yet with fervour he combined tact. How often he regretted the conduct of those, even his beloved Martyn,[9] who acted like butchers, cutting "at sin as if they did not feel any mercy for sinners"![10] Simeon knew that he that winneth souls[11] is wise, and that the best way to do so was by love.

[1] Brown, p. 176.   [2] Carus, p. 225.   [3] Cf. ibid., pp. 442, 817.
[4] Ibid., p. 429.
[5] On "brokenness" see above, Douglas Webster, "Simeon's Pastoral Theology", pp. 97-9.
[6] Brown, p. 138.   [7] Ibid., p. 10.   [8] Carus, p. 63.
[9] Brown, p. 96.   [10] Ibid., p. 106.
[11] Ibid., pp. 106, 169; Carus, pp. 65, 468.

CHARLES SIMEON

III

How did Simeon's influence spread? He himself went regularly
on preaching tours, ministering, while he was allowed to do so,
in the Church of Scotland,[1] and going on deputations for the
various societies he supported. Simeon, however, as we have
noted above, was no itinerant; his main influence in the country
was therefore an indirect one. It was exercised in two principal
ways, by the spread of "Simeonites" into livings all over England
and by the establishment of patronage interests.

Simeon's followers were not content to minister in isolation;
and after the fellowship they had enjoyed at Cambridge one can
hardly expect that they would be. They therefore gathered themselves together in clerical societies, some going to established
bodies such as the Elland Society, others founding new organiza-
tions. One such was the Matlock Bath Society [2], a body of clergymen gathered together by Philip Gell in 1816 to discuss questions
of doctrine, Church Order, and pastoralia. Gell was a friend of
Simeon, having been up at Trinity around 1800. It is not, I think,
rash to assume that the seventeen of the first twenty-five members
of the Society who had been educated at Cambridge (and were
mostly young men) must have come under Simeon's influence.
Indeed, this influence penetrated literally into the far corners of
Britain. The importance of Simeon in the Irish Evangelical
Movement, for instance, has recently been shown by Dean
Jackson.[3] Patrick Brontë was sent from Ireland to Cambridge;
and William Atthill, Prebendary of Maheraculmony, indefatigable
organizer and incomparable preacher,[4] had sat at Simeon's feet.

It is, however, with patronage[5] that I want mainly to deal in
considering the extension of Simeon's influence. The purchase
of advowsons was a means of ensuring that the Gospel was faith-
fully preached and thereby of winning souls. "I purchase spheres

[1] Carus, chs. VI, VII, especially pp. 163–4.
[2] See the present author's "Evangelical Parish Clergy, 1820–1840", *Church
Quarterly Review*, CLIX, 1958, pp. 387–95.
[3] R. W. Jackson, "Some Early Irish Evangelicals", *The Churchman*, LXXI,
1957, No. 2, pp. 58ff.
[4] Ibid., p. 62.
[5] For access to much of the material on which this section is based, I am
indebted to the Chairman and Secretary of Simeon's Trustees, Very Rev.
J. G. Tiarks, Provost of Bradford, who kindly allowed me to use the Trust
papers.

of influence," Simeon said. The idea of regarding patronage as a spiritual responsibility was new in Simeon's day, something else which he learnt from old John Thornton. The state of things in the eighteenth and early nineteenth centuries was perhaps no worse than for a long time before, but, through the work of such men as Thornton and Simeon and the writer of the *Black Books* of 1820 and 1831, corruption was shown for what it was. Simony, place-seeking, pluralism, absenteeism, these were rife and wreaked havoc on the spiritual welfare of the country. Faithful and responsible patronage sought not only to overcome such evils, but also among Evangelicals to perpetuate a fruitful ministry. Evangelicals had learnt the value of this, after seeing the efforts of Henry Venn at Huddersfield and Cadogan at Reading nullified by unsympathetic successors.

John Thornton used his wealth to buy livings, and at his death he owned nine and one presentation of another. In his Will he vested the patronage in three trustees, Bentley of Camberwell, Henry Foster, and John Venn of Little Dunham (afterwards of Clapham). In addition, he nominated nine other successor-trustees, of whom Simeon was one. Simeon succeeded in 1813 on the death of John Venn.[1] He was therefore immediately called upon to make a selection for the important living of Clapham. At the same time he was required to consider a nomination for another influential sphere, that of St Peter's, Colchester. What happened in this instance is worth recounting at some length, for it shows the principles upon which Simeon acted and the tenacity with which he sought to apply them. The trustees were beset with applications. The parishioners, the former incumbent's widow, Robert and Henry Thornton, all supported the appointment of John Bridges Storry, a young man and apparently suffering from deafness, to his father's living. Others wanted Bull, the Curate, to succeed; whilst Samuel Thornton urged the claims of Owen of Fulham. He had, however, to minimize Owen's pluralism (he held a living in Essex, besides Fulham) and to recommend that his itinerancy be restrained. ("The great objection to Mr. Owen in my mind is the habit of going about in a cause[2] highly commendable at first, but which no longer demands his peculiar exertion, &

---

[1] Simeon was not, as Canon Smyth states (*Simeon and Church Order*, p. 246), an original Thornton trustee (cf. Carus, p. 368). Moreover, the trustees were appointed under John Thornton's Will (1791), not Henry's.

[2] He was first Secretary of the Bible Society. Cf. Carus, p. 403.

he shd. be admonished to consider the care of Souls peculiarly committed to him as his first Object before he is presented to any living.") This must have been enough to disqualify him from Simeon's consideration. Simeon, however, had not only to resist petitioners but also to persuade his fellow-trustees. He wanted William Marsh to succeed; Foster supported Storry; and John King, the third trustee, seems to have doubted Marsh's acceptability as not being a "*decidedly* Evangelical character" in the terms of Thornton's Will.[1] Simeon eventually triumphed; not least, I believe, because of the light in which he portrayed to King their immense responsibility as trustees. This passage must be quoted at length:

"I conceive it was never intended to invest us with Patronage, but simply to appoint us as God's instruments for good to the people of the Parishes committed to us. The Testator conceived of us as Men of high principle and of strict integrity; incapable of being influenced by any consideration but the welfare of immortal souls and the glory of our God; Hence, in the discharge of our high *Trust*, I think that no partiality to friends, no attitude to Benefactors, no Respect to Individuals, in whatever relation they stand either to the Testator himself, or to the Parish that may be vacant, no deference to petitioners; in a word, no consideration under heaven, except that of conferring the greatest possible good on the souls of our fellow-creatures, is to influence us in our choice. The moment we suffer inferior considerations to operate on our minds, we descend from our high Station to the poor pitiful level of private Patrons. And it is of great importance for us to reflect on the difference which will be introduced thereby on our consultations. When we met together each would have some friend to serve; and thus we should be drawing different ways; but if we have no thought or wish but that of promoting God's honour, we meet, as Men of God should meet, and as the Apostles of our Lord and Saviour would have met in our circumstances."[2]

This final comparison illustrates the high regard in which Simeon held the office, one indeed by which they might advance—or retard—"the welfare of immortal souls and the glory of our God". His experience at Colchester, Darlaston (where he refused

[1] Letter of 26 January 1814 (Simeon's Trust Papers).
[2] Letter of 2 February 1814 (Simeon's Trust Papers).

Mrs Wilberforce among other petitioners)[1] and elsewhere[2] no doubt led him to include the specific warning against applications of this kind in the Solemn Charge to his own trustees, part of which reads:

"That, when they shall be called upon to appoint to a Living, they consult nothing but the welfare of the people, for whom they are to provide, and whose eternal interests have been confided to them. They must on no account be influenced by any solicitation of the great and powerful, or by any partiality towards a particular individual, or by compassion towards any one on account of the largeness of his family or the smallness of his income. They must be particularly on their guard against petitions from the parishes to be provided for. . . ."[3]

The Charge also refers to the supreme necessity of finding the right man. He constantly brought the importance of this before others, to Richardson of York on his accession to the Thornton Trust in 1814,[4] to Mrs Wilberforce (*"To obtain a fit person will not satisfy my conscience.* I must, in order to approve myself to God, have the *fittest person I can possibly find.*"[5]), to his friends, Marsh and Carr. To these latter who sought the appointment of John Charlesworth to St Peter's, Ipswich, he wrote: "Why have I bought these Livings? Not to present a good man to each, but to fill them with men who shall prove great and leading characters of commanding influence in the Church of God."[6] Piety was not enough; Simeon wanted a man "who, with his piety, combines a solid judgment and a perfectly independent mind". Simeon's candour was a great asset in choosing incumbents. He exposed the shortcomings of young Storry; and of one Bromehead he wrote to Charles Grant in headmasterly fashion: "I think he would do very well in any situation where moderate and rather slender talents will suffice."[7]

Simeon chose so carefully because upon his choice depended the eternal welfare of souls. Hence "Usefulness to the people should be the first consideration"; and thus "If it be a populous

[1] Letter of 20 July 1814 (Simeon's Trust Papers).
[2] Carus, pp. 746–7.   [3] Ibid., p. 748 n.
[4] Carus, p. 382; cf. also p. 752.
[5] Letter of 20 July 1814 (Simeon's Trust Papers).
[6] Letter of 29 April 1833 (Simeon's Trust Papers).
[7] Letter of October 1805 in the Ridley Hall Collection, and quoted by kind permission of the Principal of Ridley Hall, Rev. C. W. J. Bowles.

place, send a Boanerges." With this thought of usefulness in mind, he remarked that "The weight which a Minister obtains by long residence, is of very great Importance."[1] Even a series of like-minded men, an object he sought to attain, could not be as beneficial as the regular ministry of one man over a long period. But in what did "usefulness to the people" consist? As Canon Smyth has noted, Simeon's object was positive, characteristic of all he did; he sought to fix the gospel in a place in perpetuity.[2] "Preach the gospel" was his unfailing watchword. On preferring John Venn the younger to Hereford, he advised him to know "nothing but Christ and Him crucified. . . . Speak all that the Scripture speaks, and as the Scripture speaks it. . . . Souls are perishing for lack of knowledge."[3] Ten days later Simeon reminded Venn that he hoped "one day to join with you in singing [the new song in heavenly Zion], accompanied with a goodly number from Hereford".[4] That was how Simeon regarded souls. He counted them with the intensity of miserly acquisitiveness: "I have already above 40 Churches and Chapels—Now supposing *one* soul *pr. Ann.* more converted in every one of them than would be under a common and careless Ministry, how rich shall I be in the short space of ten or twenty years! Is not this worth a few pounds?"[5]

No wonder he spent his own considerable fortune and the sum of substantial gifts in buying advowsons. His experience of the Thornton Trust led him to purchase livings, beginning with that of Cheltenham in 1817. At his death twenty-one livings went into the Trust he founded. They included Newcastle-under-Lyme; St Peter's, Hereford; Bradford; St Giles', Northampton; St Peter's and St Margaret's, Ipswich; St Peter's, Colchester; St Dunstan's-in-the-West; and Darlaston. The last three were obtained from the Thornton Trust on its dissolution. Simeon had hoped to buy all the advowsons in that Trust, but a series of difficulties and misunderstandings arose. First, there were differences about the question whether the Trust might be dissolved. Samuel Thornton quoted a lawyer's opinion to the effect that it

---

[1] These quotations are all from the letter of October 1805 in the Ridley Hall Collection.
[2] *Simeon and Church Order*, p. 204.
[3] Carus, pp. 712–13.   [4] Ibid., p. 714.
[5] Letter to Dr Ring, 13 August 1836 (Ridley Hall Collection).

might be on the death of a trustee,[1] whereas Simeon maintained that, so long as three of old John Thornton's nominees were alive, it must continue.[2] The main trouble arose, however, as a result of two widely divergent valuations. On 5 February 1822 Thornton quoted £5,915 as a fair price, but no agreement could be reached on the annual value of the livings by which the purchase price might be fixed. A certain Mr Bailey of Royal Exchange Assurance provided a rough estimate of the value, but Simeon, precise as always, wrote to Samuel Thornton: "It will be more satisfactory to both of us to proceed on grounds actually ascertained, than of those which are purely conjectural. And I trust it will be a source of mutual joy to us to perpetuate the pious designs of your honoured Father, in whose footsetps I shd. account it my highest honour to tread."[3] Whether Thornton shared this desire the subsequent history of the affair may give us leave to doubt. On 4 March 1822 Bailey produced his revised estimate—£9,707! Simeon was astounded, but felt that, having asked for the second estimate, he was bound to accept it. He appears to have given some sort of verbal acceptance to Thornton in the presence of the latter's nephew, J. T. Leslie Melville. A friend, however, advised him that he was not bound to accept. He therefore saw Thornton again and, believing himself discharged from his obligation, reinvested the money he had drawn. Then Thornton made two offers of all the livings except Bisley and Chobham for £6,000 or all except Roach [Roche (Cornwall)] for £7,000; but negotiations broke down. On 11 March Thornton wrote to Simeon a letter on which the latter has noted: "Mr. T. still insisting on the purchase with a *menace*." The *menace* lies in the last sentence: "I yet hope you will not abandon and compell me to adopt measures that must be unpleasant to us both." On the next day Melville wrote upbraiding Simeon: "I am at a loss to imagine upon what Christian principle you can justify the breach of an engagement you are bound in honour to perform." Melville's part in all this seems to have been shabbier even than that of Thornton. He had acted as intermediary between Thornton and the valuer, Bailey, and admitted before Simeon that he had revealed to Bailey his personal interest in the matter, "*but that he*

---

[1] Letter of 12 February 1822 (Simeon's Trust Papers).
[2] Letter of 18 February 1822 (Simeon's Trust Papers).
[3] Letter of 12 February 1822 (Simeon's Trust Papers).

must not regard that in the Estimate". Nevertheless (again on Melville's report) "when he told Mr. Bailey about the change of ground for the Estimate from one life of 39 to that of two out of four Trustees, Mr. Bailey said, '*O that will make an immense difference*' ".[1] After reading such passages as this, the insertion in the passage quoted above of "Christian" before "principle" over a caret-mark seems to tell us quite a lot about Melville. Simeon, however, was not to be browbeaten. Indeed, as he put it in the affidavit quoted above, he "still, for love sake, continued to solicit, rather than demand, a Release from the engagement".[2] On 15 March Thornton proposed arbitration by a common friend. Then there arose new difficulties about the choice of arbitrators. Eventually the matter was referred, in New Testament fashion, to the judgement of fellow-believers, in this case Wilberforce, Stephen, and Lord Teignmouth. To them Simeon presented the affidavit already mentioned, and asked whether in honour or in conscience he was obliged to buy the livings. On 18 May the verdict was given in Simeon's favour. Thornton granted release and regretted the misunderstanding that had arisen.

Thus prevented from making a major accession to his Trust, Simeon purchased livings quietly over the years. His next large opportunity came with the passing of the Corporation Act of 1835, by which municipal corporations were compelled to sell livings in their gift. Most of Simeon's own money was gone, but an appeal brought in several thousand pounds. Simeon wished to subscribe on a fifty-fifty basis with local support, but there was little response in this way. To Miss Evans of Darley he wrote: "Alas! if the people of Warwick, or Worcester, or Shrewsbury, or Bath have no more zeal and love than the people of Derby."[3] He wanted to buy the advowsons of all the provincial towns.[4] In fact, of those mentioned in the letter quoted above he secured only Bath[5] and Derby.[6] He had lost opportunities before, in 1827, for instance, when he failed to get Harrogate and, a place he knew, "all that

---

[1] Simeon's Affidavit on the dispute (Simeon's Trust Papers).

[2] Ibid., p. 7v.

[3] Letter of 9 March 1836 (Simeon's Trust Papers).

[4] Smyth, *Simeon and Church Order*, 1940, pp. 202–3, quoting a letter in *The British Magazine*, Vol. IX, 1836, pp. 549–50.

[5] Bath with its five chapels cost Simeon £6,300.

[6] The local subscriptions for Derby were collected by Philip Gell, and the sum of £400 included gifts from fellow-members of the Matlock Bath Clerical Society.

immensely important Town of Preston[1] in Lancashire with 4 Chapels and 30,000 Souls, and must leave the field to Papists".[2] But 1836 provided an opportunity that would not be repeated and could not therefore be missed. In the event, he and his successors acquired, besides Bath and Derby, Macclesfield, Bridlington, St Thomas's and St Martin's in Liverpool, and Beverley Minster. This last was bought against the bids of the Duke of Northumberland, and Simeon was later asked by Dikes of Hull to sell it to the Duke. His reply is further testimony to his high sense of responsibility. After pointing out that he was not free to sell since he acted not for himself but as the agent of those who subscribed, he continued: "And I am God's Agent also; and have bought the souls of that place for *him*—What account should I give *to him* at his judgment seat, if with my views of the worth of a Gospel Ministry, I should deprive them of it after having secured [it] for them. What are Dukes or Kings in comparison of fidelity to God?"[3]

The importance of the kind of sphere which Simeon sought cannot be better illustrated than by a description of what happened at Bradford. Between 1801 and 1841 the population increased from 29,754 to 105,259. In 1843 there were fourteen churches or chapels, of which five had been built in the few years of the very active Dr Scoresby's incumbency. In the four years from 1839 to 1843 the number of schools rose from one to nine, and there were plans for twelve more. Archdeacon Hodson seems to have been rather niggardly of praise when he reported to his fellow-trustees: "With many things to regret in the progress of measures since his appointment, my decided impression is that a man possessed of less than his energy, firmness and constancy would have been quite unequal to bear up against the multiplied difficulties & discouragements wh. have been opposed to his efforts."[4] I think Scoresby would have satisfied Simeon's requirements; he seems to have been a Boanerges.

In seeking places such as Bradford (though this came into the Trust before the 1835 Act) Simeon was acting with prophetic

---

[1] "An immense sphere"—Carus, p. 514. Roger Carus Wilson was vicar at the time of Simeon's visit in 1819.

[2] Letter to Mrs Evans, 30 March 1827 (Simeon's Trust Papers).

[3] Letter of 31 August 1836 (Simeon's Trust Papers).

[4] Simeon's Trust Memoranda.

foresight. He recognized, as only Bishop Sumner of Chester[1] seems to have done in that day, the ecclesiastical implications of the increasing urban growth in England. This was but part of that acute sense of practical issues which was such a pillar of Simeon's ecclesiastical statesmanship. He gave to this patronage work his money, his energy, his time (witness his tours of his churches), and his practical wisdom. The product of his own fervour and generosity he passed on to his trustees, men carefully selected, who over long years of service[2] diligently nurtured and extended what they had received from a man who had been to them truly a father in God. They in their turn passed on their trust, and the work continues, an abiding testimony to one man's vision, determination and, to use Simeon's own phrase, "fidelity to God".

IV

Simeon's influence abroad[3] was no less, some would say greater, than it was at home. It was a three-fold interest—India, the Church Missionary Society, and the Jews—taken up in that order. The needs of India were recognized on the spot by Charles Grant, a Scotsman[4] in the service of the East India Company. He bought a church in Calcutta and there David Brown ministered from 1790 to his death in 1812. Brown knew Simeon from his Cambridge days, and to the young don of thirty appeals were soon made for help. Thus began Simeon's long association with India, as a result of which there went out to that vast field of evangelism a succession of chaplains, Martyn, Thomason, and Corrie chief among them, sustained by Simeon's prayers, and followed and encouraged by his continual interest in their work. The correspondence of Simeon and Thomason is a lesson in spiritual fatherly care and interest.

[1] J. B. Sumner, later Archbishop of Canterbury. During his twenty years at Chester (1828-48) 138 new churches were consecrated in the diocese, which then comprised the whole of Lancashire and Cheshire.

[2] Of the first five trustees, William Carus (the biographer of Simeon and his successor at Trinity Church, Cambridge) served till 1890, John Venn of Hereford till 1878, and William Marsh of Colchester till 1864.

[3] In this section I am considerably indebted to Michael Hennell's *John Venn and the Clapham Sect*, 1958, ch. 5.

[4] Scotsmen played a prominent part in the Evangelical Revival in the Church of England. Amongst leading figures there were Stephen and Macaulay, and in Liverpool the elder Gladstone and General Murray.

Neither Parliament nor the East India Company would allow missionaries to enter India. As a result men went to India as chaplains to the British community in the East India Company, but engaged in work among the natives as well. No such restraints, however, could be placed on missionary endeavour elsewhere, and the interest in forwarding efforts of this nature was such that in the last decade of the eighteenth century no less than five societies were founded. Of these none has been more influential than the last, the Church Missionary Society, established in 1799. Many Anglicans who wished to support missionary work were dissatisfied with the limited and lukewarm endeavours of the Society for the Propagation of the Gospel on the one hand and with the interdenominational principle of the London Missionary Society (1795) on the other. For them a solution was provided by the inception of the Society for Missions to Africa and the East, to use C.M.S.'s original title.

There are two views of Simeon's part in the discussions which led to the establishment of the Society. One is Mr Hennell's: "In all these discussions one figure stands out—Charles Simeon";[1] the other is that of Charles Hole who blamed Simeon for the delay that occurred between the London Eclectic Society's discussion in 1796 of the question, "With what propriety, and in what mode, can a mission be attempted to the heathen from the Established Church?"[2] and the Society's foundation in 1799. Hole asserted that despair and indecision resulted from "the form in which Mr. Simeon put his question, when he asked about a mission 'from the Established Church', suggesting 'the corporate body of the Church of England, with the bishops at the head' ".[3] Simeon no doubt would have preferred this, but it is, I think, unjust to claim this as the reason for delay.[4] In some directions Simeon approved of interdenominational co-operation,[5] but here, with John Venn, Simeon knew the need of Church Order, of the "Church principle".[6] In fact, far from delaying the new venture, Simeon urged it forward. He was present at both the Rauceby and Elland Society's meetings in 1795 to discuss the use of Jane's

---

[1] *John Venn and the Clapham Sect*, 1958, p. 216. [2] Carus, p. 111.
[3] *The Early History of the Church Missionary Society*, 1898, p. 26.
[4] See the summary of the whole discussion—Carus, p. 111.
[5] Cf., e.g. his letter to *The Record* on accommodating the beliefs and practices of Quakers and Socinians in the Bible Society, *The British and Foreign Bible Society Controversy*, 1831. [6] See Hennell, op. cit., p. 233.

legacy of £4,000 for this purpose.[1] He pressed for action continually in the years that followed, and at the crucial meeting of the Eclectic Society on 18 March 1799 he proposed three questions: "*What can we do?—When shall we do it?—How shall we do it?*"[2], and answered them thus: "We require something more than resolutions. . . . Directly. . . . It is hopeless to wait for Missionaries. Send out Catechists."[2] On 12 April at the Castle and Falcon Inn, Aldersgate Street, the Society was founded. Thus did Simeon realize the need, thus was he urged on by his realization of it, and thus did he grasp even the smallest opportunities that might forward the purpose which he served. This, however, was but the beginning. In the years ahead he inspired scores of men to dedicate themselves as missionaries for the Society which he had done as much as any to bring into being.

The strongest evangelistic interest of Simeon's later life was, however, the conversion of the Jews. He looked for a full and imminent[3] restoration of God's chosen people. He preached for it diligently, and with what enthusiasm he wrote to Thomason about this work! From 1813 onwards[4] his correspondence is studded with references to it. In 1815 the Jews' Society passed into the hands of a committee consisting entirely of Anglicans. Notable among its leaders was Lewis Way, not least of whose achievements was the securing of a protocol from the rulers at the Aix Conference in 1818, "applauding his views, and engaging to exert themselves in their respective empires for the temporal and spiritual good of the Jews".[5] Whilst Way and others evangelized on the Continent, Simeon at home acted as a kind of one-man general staff, preaching for the Society, recruiting workers, spreading propaganda, collecting funds, advising on overall strategy. He did so with even more than his usual sense of urgency. He lived to see the work prosper remarkably. An annual income of £7,000 in 1815 was doubled by 1836. Episcopal patronage was bestowed on the Society. The New Testament was translated into Hebrew, and this and cheap copies of the Hebrew Old Testament were widely circulated. The Society's activities were extended to Eastern and South Eastern Europe, Asia Minor, Jerusalem, and North West Africa. In that progress Charles Simeon had no mean part.

[1] Carus, p. 107.　　　　　[2] Ibid., p. 169.　　　　　[3] Ibid., p. 514.
[4] Ibid., p. 364　　　　　[5] Ibid., p. 501.

V

We come then to the end of Simeon's life, and with it we return to his beloved Cambridge, scene of sorrows and of triumphs. Violent opposition was now only a memory. Men like John Sargent who once had scoffed were now at his side.[1] Old Henry Venn had spoken the truth, probably more fully then he knew, when in 1783 he wrote to Riland: "Cambridge is going to be in a ferment—Mr. Simeon's ministry is likely to be blessed."[2] After the winds and storms there came a long and fruitful summer. In 1818 Simeon wrote to Thomason: "As for the Gownsmen, never was anything like what they are at this day. I am forced to let them go up into the galleries, which I never suffered before; and notwithstanding that, multitudes of them are forced to stand in the aisles for want of a place to sit down."[3] And within a few months of his death Simeon could testify that not only did this continue, but that senior members of the University, many of them probably undergraduate disciples of former days, were like-minded with him in the faith. Much of this state of affairs he attributed with his characteristic generosity to his assistant and biographer, William Carus; but here he was surely too generous. Such was this success that, he told Rev. E. B. Elliott, "a most influential head of one of the Colleges congratulated me the other day on having lived to see the triumph of my own principles. Truly this is a ground for thankfulness to Almighty God, far beyond any other blessing that could have been vouchsafed to me."[4] With that blessing and in that thankfulness Simeon was soon to end his earthly course.

He succeeded beyond Cambridge because he succeeded in Cambridge. This man "who, more than any other, inspired and promoted the Evangelical Revival in the second and third generations of its course"[5] was known, respected, listened to, and followed. At the end of one sermon he urged his audience to "cry mightily to God that the cruse of salt may be cast into this fountain [Cambridge] from whence so many streams are issuing; that being rendered salubrious they may fertilize this whole land, and

---

[1] Ibid., p. 92.   [2] Ibid., p. 47.   [3] Ibid., p. 496.
[4] Letter of 2 May 1836 (Simeon's Trust Papers).
[5] Smyth, *Simeon and Church Order*, 1940, p. 19.

be the means of diffusing life and salvation to the remotest corners of the globe".[1] God heard the cry and gave the blessing. Simeon's authority was tremendous. Men consulted him about the education of their sons; clergymen and patrons sought his advice about curates.[2] But the importance of his practical advice was as nothing beside the value of the spiritual counsel which he gave to countless inquirers. His friendship covered every class of society, from earls and bishops to the poor woman on her death-bed who taught him a valuable lesson.[3]

The influence of the upper-middle-class was dominant over all others in the Victorian era, and to that many important Evangelicals belonged from the members of Clapham Sect onwards. For these and their successors Charles Simeon was a respected name and his words a revered message. These men and women lived their lives in the ever-present consciousness of an all-seeing and all-judging God, and to this may be traced in not insignificant measure the sense of political responsibility, commercial integrity, social philanthropy, and moral purity which pervaded the nineteenth century. Simeon used to say that Martyn seemed to speak to him out of his picture saying, " 'Be serious—Be in earnest—Don't trifle—don't trifle'. Then smiling at the picture and gently bowing, he added: 'And I won't trifle—I won't trifle.' "[4] That sums up the Evangelical's attitude—"Be in earnest"; and out of it there came uncompromising honesty, a high sense of duty, a passion for self-improvement, a rigorous

---

[1] Sermon 359—"Elijah Healing the Spring with a Cruse of Salt."
[2] Cf. the elder Gladstone's visit in 1816 by which John Jones was invited to St Andrew's, Liverpool, and Rawson went to St Thomas', Seaforth [Note: W. E. Gladstone said wrongly that Jones went to Seaforth—Morley, *Life of Gladstone*, 1904, p. 11]. Jones had wanted to go into the mission field but met parental opposition (Letters of 21 October and 4 November 1814—Ridley Hall Collection). He eventually became Archdeacon of Liverpool (1855-87) and died in 1889, an example of how long some of Simeon's disciples exercised an active ministry.
[3] Viz., "May not our own weight of glory also be greatly increased, by a due improvement of our light and momentary afflictions? Is not this last consideration alone sufficient to reconcile us to a prolonging of our troubles, and a deferring of our heavenly felicity?"—Sermon 460—"Impatience Reproved", and note.
[4] Cf. N. G. Annan, *Leslie Stephen*, 1951—"Each day [Henry] Thornton examines his life according to the Commandments laid upon him by God's Book. Has he lived according to the Law? How can he amend his acts to follow it more closely?"—p. 115.

critical spirit,[1] immense industry, thrift, sobriety, restraint, and asceticism.

This is no place to examine in detail the Evangelical contribution to the English character, but two of its achievements must be mentioned. Of one, it has been claimed that "the influence of the Evangelical Revival on the Public School system was among its most important and most permanent contributions to English life".[2] One cannot ignore the work of men such as Butler, Arnold, Moberly, and Christopher Wordsworth, none of whom was an Evangelical. Nevertheless, Evangelicals had their part in reforming the older public schools (Simeon himself criticized his old school, Eton, in a letter to the Provost,[3] and J. I. Welldon, a Cambridge Evangelical, did great work at Tonbridge[4]) and in founding new ones.[5] Moreover, the moral values upon which the nineteenth-century public-schools laid so much stress were reinforced by the atmosphere of the Evangelical home, the second achievement (if I may call it such) to which I must refer. Speaking of his own home G. W. E. Russell, who cast off his Evangelical allegiance, wrote: "To these parents I look back with loving and grateful reverence, and I recall an abiding sense of religious responsibility, a self-sacrificing energy in works of mercy, an evangelistic zeal, an aloofness from the world, and a level of saintliness in daily life, such as I do not expect again to see realized on earth."[6] *There* is a fine achievement, and nothing of degenerate Evangelicalism, its formalism, hypocrisy, soulless rigours, and sometimes morbid sense of sin, none of this can take away from that wonderful and very practical beauty of holiness which marked the zenith of Evangelical living. In this Evangelical attainment Charles Simeon was no mean influence for good. Moreover, such a standard of private life inevitably affected standards of public

[1] Annan (op. cit., p. 110) writes: "How many of the middle-class intellectual aristocracy are reared in Evangelical families!" and supports his statement with a massive array of evidence.

[2] J. Marlowe, *The Puritan Tradition in English Life*, 1956, p. 106.

[3] Carus, p. 609.

[4] He "brought to his work at Tonbridge strong views of right and wrong, good classical scholarship, firm methods of discipline, and sound administrative experience.... He preached as he spoke, with a directness that was perhaps not eloquent, but that came straight from the heart, and so reached the hearts of his hearers".—S. Rivington, *Tonbridge School*, 1898, pp. 223–4.

[5] Francis Close, for instance, Simeon's nominee at Cheltenham, helped to found Cheltenham College.

[6] *The Household of Faith*, 1902, pp. 231–2.

life. Evangelicals united a high awareness of stewardship and accountability to God with an intense love of souls. From this derived their impetus to social endeavours. Men like Wilberforce and Shaftesbury were raised up to accomplish what, under God, they did; but behind them was a mass of public opinion, without which they could have done nothing and in the creation of which the Evangelicals as a whole, and Charles Simeon not a little, played by far the greatest part. His followers, through the years, in cures of every kind, in city-slums and quiet villages, worked out and showed the social implications of the Gospel. Lay "Sims" brought their influence to bear in every aspect of the national life, in Parliament, local government and philanthropy, in the Army, commercial and administrative services, right to the far corners of the globe.[1] Laymen and clerics together led men to refuse to tolerate the evils which nineteenth-century reform destroyed. As in those last months of his life Simeon thanked God for what had come to pass, he might well have done so, too, for what was yet to be.

His work and influence continue still. One might construct a kind of genealogical tree, and show how to his work with undergraduates the Cambridge Inter-Collegiate Christian Union, the Inter-Varsity Fellowship, and the Student Christian Movement may trace their origin, and how from that work also the China Inland Mission and the Keswick Convention in turn take their rise; how again his missionary endeavours were important in that line which includes the Church Missionary Society, the Bible Churchmen's Missionary Society, the Church Missions to Jews, and the British and Foreign Bible Society; and how his patronage interests are still exemplified in his own and other Evangelical trusts.

Charles Simeon was dominated always by a two-fold concern— the glory of God and the love of souls. To these ends he delighted to minister in the Church he loved so well. He is not just a figure of history; he is a living influence. While we honour his memory, may we who follow him continue to profit by his example and, with God's help, advance the work to which he dedicated all he was and had.

[1] Warren, *Charles Simeon*, 1949, p. 30.

Select Bibliography

C. SIMEON, *Horae Homileticae: or Discourses*, 21 vols., 1832–33.

H. VENN, *Life and a selection from the Letters of the late Rev. Henry Venn*, 1834.

F. CLOSE, *A Brief Sketch of the Character and Last Days of Charles Simeon*, 1836.

The Christian Observer, January, April, and May, 1837.

M. M. PRESTON, *Memoranda of the Rev. Chas. Simeon*, 1840.

W. CARUS, *Memoirs of the Life of the Rev. Charles Simeon*, 1847.

J. WILLIAMSON, *A Brief Memoir of the Rev. Chas. Simeon*, 1848.

H. GUNNING, *Reminiscences of the University, Town and County of Cambridge*, 1855.

A. W. BROWN, *Recollections of the Conversation Parties of the Rev. Chas. Simeon*, 1863.

W. CARUS, *Extracts from Simeon's Memoirs on the Composition and Delivery of Sermons*, 1887.

H. NOEL, *Charles Simeon of Cambridge*, 1890.

H. C. G. MOULE, *Charles Simeon*, 1892 (republished by Inter-Varsity Fellowship, 1948).

C. H. SIMPKINSON, *Typical English Churchmen*, 1902, pp. 257–95.

J. VENN, *Annals of a Clerical Family*, 1904.

D. A. WINSTANLEY, *Unreformed Cambridge*, 1935.

Charles Simeon, An Interpretation, Centenary Addresses delivered at Cambridge, 1936.

CHARLES SMYTH, *Simeon and Church Order*, 1940.

CHARLES SMYTH, *The Art of Preaching*, 1940.

M. A. C. WARREN, *Charles Simeon*, 1949.

F. D. COGGAN, "Great Preachers—IV. Charles Simeon", *Theology*, April 1951.

D. WEBSTER, "Charles Simeon and the Liturgy", *Theology*, August 1951.

M. L. LOANE, *Cambridge and the Evangelical Succession*, 1952.

M. HENNELL, *John Venn and the Clapham Sect*, 1958.

J. WALSH, "Magdalene Evangelicals", *Church Quarterly Review*, October–December, 1958.

Dictionary of National Biography, vol. LII, pp. 255–7.

Index

(References to doctrines, etc., relate to Simeon's views thereon, except where otherwise stated or where an entry is marked with an asterisk.)